THE REHABILITATION OF FREUD

BAKHTIN AND OTHERS

THE REHABILITATION
OF FREUD

BAKHTIN AND OTHERS

Two Novellas
by
Victor Beilis

TRANSLATED FROM THE RUSSIAN,

WITH AN INTRODUCTION AND AFTERWORD

BY

Richard B. Grose

OTHER

OTHER PRESS
New York

"Reabilitatsia Freida" ("The Rehabilitation of Freud") and "Bakhtin i drugie" ("Bakhtin and Others") copyright © 1992 by Victor Beilis

Translation and editorial materials copyright © 2002 by Richard B. Grose

Production Editor: Robert D. Hack

This book was set in 11½ pt. Adobe Caslon by Alpha Graphics of Pittsfield, NH.

10 9 8 7 6 5 4 3 2 1

Library of Congress Cataloging-in-Publication Data

Beilis, V. A. (Viktor Aleksandrovich)
  [Reabilitatsiia Freida. English]
  The rehabilitation of Freud ; Bakhtin and others: two novellas / by Victor Beilis ; translated from the Russian, with an introduction and an afterword by Richard B. Grose.
    p. cm.
  Includes bibliographical references.
  ISBN 1-59051-029-1
  I. Title: Rehabilitation of Freud ; Bakhtin and others; two novellas. II. Beilis, V. A. (Viktor Aleksandrovich). Bakhtin i drugie. English. III. Title: Bakhtin and others: two novellas. IV. Title.

PG3479.3.I43 R413 2002
891.73'44—dc21

2002025784

These translations are dedicated

to the memory of

Vera S. Dunham (1912–2001)

CONTENTS

ACKNOWLEDGMENTS

This translation of "The Rehabilitation of Freud" owes much to the assistance of its dedicatee, the late Vera S. Dunham, who in 1994 read an early draft and sent it back to me fully marked up. Vera was born near Moscow in 1912, received her graduate education in Europe in the 1930s, and had a distinguished career in the U.S. as a Slavicist. She died in March 2001, before she could learn that the translation she had corrected so carefully had just been accepted for publication and that it would be dedicated to her. In making the final revisions of the translation several months after her death, I consulted that 1994 marked-up copy and was struck again by the care and sharp intelligence she had expended on it. Rereading her many comments, I felt her living presence in the room.

Her love of the two languages, her respect for the art of translation, and her determination to see it gotten right were palpable on every page. I hope I may be forgiven one quotation from her written comments (which accompanied, as I must add here, many corrections of errors and suggestions for improvements). In a margin she wrote, "I have spent now more than half an hour meditating as to what to do with this key word, *naklikat'*. . . you did the right thing, the only possible solution, methinks." All who knew her will recognize Vera's inimitable personality in this comment. And I believe her. I can see her right now, sitting in her house in Port Jefferson, looking out the window through the trees onto Long Island Sound, and thinking for half an hour about the various ways to translate *naklikat'*. The difficult circumstances of her final years, sadly, prevented her from correcting "Bakhtin and Others." Although I hope the absence of her work on that story is not noticeable to readers, I know that the result would have been better if she had felt up to it. She is missed.

Victor Beilis has been uniformly helpful and encouraging throughout the process of preparing these translations for publication. From our first letters, exchanged in 1994 after I tracked him down in Germany, through our e-mails in recent years, it has given me nothing but pleasure to work with him.

Eleanor Johnson helped greatly by pointing out the many points in the translations where I had not brought the language the entire distance from Russian to colloquial English, and by giving the essay a careful, critical reading.

Finally, my thanks to Dr. Carol Bandini and Nicole Potter for taking time out from their busy schedules to read parts of the manuscript and share their reactions with me.

TRANSLATOR'S INTRODUCTION

The two stories in this volume, "The Rehabilitation of Freud" and "Bakhtin and Others," were written by Victor Beilis, in Moscow, in 1980–1981 and 1985–1986, respectively. The author is a prominent scholar of African culture, who during the 1980s, in addition to producing a steady stream of scholarly publications, was also writing fiction. This brief introduction precedes the stories to acquaint American readers with some of the intellectual and social background of these works, which come to us from the doubly removed world of Soviet Russia.

FREUD IN RUSSIA:
ACCEPTANCE, MURDER, AND REHABILITATION

The title of the story "The Rehabilitation of Freud" refers to perhaps the central topic of intellectual discussion in Soviet Russia in 1980–1981, namely that for the first time in fifty years in the Soviet Union, Freud and psychoanalysis could be publicly discussed in a positive light. To better understand this moment—and what it meant to contemporary readers of the story—it will be useful to recount the salient features of the complex history of psychoanalysis in Russia. This history has been well told twice in English: by the Russian literary scholar Alexander Etkind, in *Eros of the Impossible* (1997), and by the American historian Martin Miller, in *Freud and the Bolsheviks* (1998).

When they began being widely discussed in the first decade of the 20th century, Freud's ideas encountered much less initial resistance in Russia than in any other European country. Religious tradition as well as literary and philosophical fashion made the educated elites receptive to fundamental psychoanalytic ideas. The Russian Orthodox Church regarded faith as a matter more of feeling than of doctrine. For this reason, and because the Orthodox Church never achieved the institutional status of the Roman Catholic Church, religious leaders in Russia were less inclined to condemn the Freudian insight into the importance of sexual life for mental health. The prevailing literary fashion in Russia, Symbolism, implicated a search for "the other world" of Truth or Beauty lying beyond the visible one; in this context, psychoanalysis at first seemed to many but another way out of the fallen world. Uninhibited sex was a theme of many popular Russian novels of the time, often advocated as an expression of a pseudo-Nietzschean ideal of creative self-expression—there simply has never been the same degree of prudery in Russia as in the West. Finally, in philosophy, Nietzsche's works themselves, with their challenge to established morality, were at the height of their popularity, so Freud's implicit and explicit critique of late Victorian society had an effective forerunner. Hence Russian intellectual society was far more open to Freud's assertions about a hidden world of thoughts and feeling, largely sexual, that is present in all people and that can be accessed through a therapeutic technique in which moral constraints on verbalizations are counterproductive. Etkind goes further and argues that as a result of these and other cultural factors, Russians generally live closer to their unconscious than do Western Europeans and suffer less from repression.

The generally greater openness to psychoanalytic ideas among Russian intellectuals can be seen in the following facts. The first translation of *Interpretation of Dreams* was into Russian in 1904. The Moscow Psychoanalytic Society was founded in 1911, making it the second psychoanalytic society, after Vienna. Moscow was the site of only the third psychoanalytic training institute in Europe, after Vienna and Berlin, founded in 1922. Finally, a major theoretical contribution to psychoanalysis originated in Russia: the doctrine of the death instinct was first elaborated by the Russian psychoanalyst Sabina Spielrein.

In the years immediately after coming to power in 1917, the Bolshevik regime acted in concert with this generally positive reception; there was considerable governmental support for Freudian ideas in the first years of the Soviet regime. In the early 1920s, the Soviet government for several years supported a school that was run on the basis of psychoanalytic ideas. In addition, Freud was a frequent subject in serious intellectual journals, and attempts were made to link the theories of psychoanalysis and Marxism, thus bringing together a force for personal liberation with a force for social liberation. However, beginning about 1925, the fortunes of psychoanalysis began to decline in Russia in inverse proportion to the increasing power of Stalin. By 1930, the Soviet Union had been transformed from a revolutionary state into a totalitarian one, and psychoanalysis had been officially reinterpreted. No longer an important, fruitful discovery in the field of psychology, it was now a dangerous, misguided ideological expression of the dying European bourgeoisie. The end of open discussion of Freud was marked in 1930 with the convening of a Congress on Human Behavior; here, psychoanalysis was subjected to the same witch-hunting rhetoric with which all elements of Soviet life not under the personal control of Stalin were to be treated.

From 1930 until Stalin's death in 1953, it was fatal to a career in psychiatry to mention psychoanalysis in any but the most dismissive of terms. Nevertheless, as Miller shows, even during this period there was psychotherapy of a sort in Russia, and there is some evidence that working psychotherapists made use of Freud's work, albeit silently. After the Great Leader's death, however, the situation gradually eased. Miller shows how, gradually, the dismissals of Freud took on a covertly appreciative function. In contrast to the purveyors of blanket denunciations of previous decades, the writers now had actually read Freud and were taking the trouble to refute the theory in some detail. During the 60s, although Freudianism was still being dismissed in Russia as unscientific and mystical, the dismissals grew in depth and detail and they conveyed more and more information about the dismissed theory. The fact that Freudian theory was important enough to refute in detail signaled to younger psychiatrists that the theory was also important enough to be used, as long as one did not speak too loudly about it. This process of at first silent and then more public rehabilitation culminated in the view, widely accepted by the 1970s, that Freud—despite his many mistakes—had given the profession important, even essential theoretical insights. To discuss and ratify this change, another major scientific conference was held in 1979, virtually undoing the one in 1930.

This conference, entitled the First International Symposium on the Unconscious, was held in Tbilisi, Georgia, on October 1–6, 1979. American, European, and Soviet professionals discussed clinical and theoretical issues relating to the unconscious. Although important differences among them emerged, the very fact that such a conference could occur confirmed the sea change that had taken place in Soviet intellectual life. Although official permission to publish Freud's works and openly espouse Freudian ideas would have to wait until the end of the 1980s when glasnost made it possible, 1980 still marked a significant turning point in the history of psychoanalysis in Russia. Freud, as a permissible topic of conversation, as a great man of psychology, and as the provider of indispensable theoretical tools for psychotherapists, had been rehabilitated.

MIKHAIL MIKHAILOVICH BAKHTIN

As the title "The Rehabilitation of Freud" links that story to the long history of psychoanalysis in Russia (and to the history of Soviet "rehabilitations"), so the title "Bakhtin and Others" links that story to the highly influential work of Mikhail Mikhailovich Bakhtin (1895–1975), the literary critic-cum-philosopher, who accomplished the virtually unequaled feat of being intellectually productive under every Russian leader from Czar Nicholas II to Leonid Brezhnev.

Since the ideas of M. M. Bakhtin are important to the central character in Beilis's story, it will be useful to survey some of the main ones briefly. (So that the confusions of identity in the story not leak into this introduction, I will follow Beilis and refer to the famous writer as "M. M. Bakhtin" and to the character as "Bakhtin.") At the core of the multifarious work of M. M. Bakhtin is the notion of the relation of I and Other.[1] In this relation, the mediating process is dialogue, perhaps the term with which M. M. Bakhtin is most closely associated. A fundamental thought in the work of M. M. Bakhtin is that the self can only become a self through relating to another self, that is, in dialogue. He argued against the presumption of most Western philosophy (e.g., Descartes, Kant) that the unit of epistemological or ethical analysis is the individual, taken in isolation from others. He insisted that neither ethics nor knowledge

1. I have based my account to a large extent on that of A. Etkind in *Eros of the Impossible.*

5

can exist apart from dialogue. My acts only take on meaning in relation to others' acts, and my knowledge arises only in response to
the knowledge of others. For M. M. Bakhtin, a philosophy based
solely on the productions of single minds, and disregarding the context of the dialogue that alone gives them meaning, is fallacious. Since
the self cannot become a self in isolation, M. M. Bakhtin concluded
that we get our selves from others. In order to be me, I need the
other.

SOVIET RUSSIAN SOCIETY

Although both of these stories focus on the inner lives of their major
characters, the outer—Soviet—world is assumed, although it is not
thematicized. That world makes itself felt in details that come to
American readers from a culture that is removed from theirs both
in space and time. For example, in "The Rehabilitation of Freud,"
several important early scenes take place in the baths. This institution, important for centuries in Russia, is a place where men and
women gather for the combined purposes of cleanliness, relaxation,
and socializing. Strictly segregated by sex, the baths are also a place
where the generations freely intermingle, which is important at a certain point to Volodya, the young man who is the hero of the story.
Long-since defunct Soviet currency laws are briefly alluded to when
Volodya's father plans to buy a new apartment "for hard currency."
This reflects a specific and limited period in Soviet history. Before the
early 1970s, mere possession of foreign currency could mean prison or
death. After that, and before all restrictions on foreign currency were
lifted with the end of the Soviet Union itself, in 1991, there was a group
of privileged persons who had legal access to foreign currency, although
this was still not available to most Soviet citizens.

Volodya himself works in an "institute," we are not told of
what kind. This ubiquitous Soviet intellectual institution, a state-

sponsored think tank, provided a comfortable living for many intellectuals and professionals, as it does for our hero, who tries to solve the puzzles of his inner life while working there. Finally, the political culture of the Soviet Union makes its presence felt in a passing mention of "communal Saturday labor." In communal Saturday labor, "subbotnik" in Russian, workers and students would "voluntarily" give up one Saturday a month to work for the State without pay. This institution was begun by Lenin in the 1920s to increase popular participation in the revolution, but by 1980 it was held in contempt by most people in the country, even though they usually complied with this official expectation.

In "Bakhtin and Others," the protagonist, a Moscow literary scholar, plans to spend the summer in a rented room in a summer house ("dacha" in Russian) in order to work on an article. His wish to work outside the city in the summer reflects the virtually universal practice of Russians to spend as much time as possible during the summer "at the dacha." Thus his renting a room, although determined by his professional aims, makes him a typical Moscovite. His profession, literary studies, elicits envy from his host family, the Pavlovs. Furthermore, as a specialist in 19th-century Russian literature, he is an expert in one of the crown jewels of Russian culture, the great novels of the 19th-century prose masters. The awe in which the family immediately holds him reflects this profound respect for their literature that is typical of educated Russians. In Russia yet today, the great novels of Tolstoy and Dostoyevsky—whose full names figure prominently in the story, incidentally—represent a shared cultural heritage in a way that has no parallel in modern American culture.

These stories, written in the last decade of the Soviet Union, are linked by the theme of individuation. Separation from that which blocks individuation is the goal of both major characters, Volodya and Bakhtin. For Volodya, the blocking force is his overwhelming love for his mother, or rather his adherence to the image of her in his soul. For Bakhtin, the blocking force is the hypnotic effect of a family with whom he spends the summer, and the culture they represent. Reading these stories now, more than a decade after the end of the Soviet Union, we can think of them, within their Russian context, as powerful inquiries into the binding forces that operate in Russian culture, opposing individuation. In this reading, we can think of them as inquiries into the meaning of freedom against the background of the specific Russian challenges to it.

On the other hand, we can also read these stories, just as we continue to read the Russian classics themselves, as explorations of the meaning of freedom in a general human context. Perhaps the very fact that a Russian writer does not approach the subject of individuation from within a centuries-old tradition of the "free individual" gives him a certain, well, freedom in posing his question. For Victor Beilis in these stories, the freedom that matters is the one we have, or don't have, within our very selves.

THE REHABILITATION OF FREUD
(SKETCH FOR A NOVEL)

𝒱olodya was 14 when his mother impetuously divorced his father in order immediately to enter a new marriage. He was a quiet, secretive boy, but there was already roaming through his body a hot, exhausting fluid that at times almost seemed to scald him. He would become embarrassed and turn his face away if anyone looked at him during those moments when the hot wave rose in him. He was ashamed of these states, which he ascribed to the peculiar depravity of his imagination.

Volodya survived the rupture of his parents' marriage easily, and there was no question with whom he would live; he chose his mother. At first, his mother's divorce and remarriage were for him ordinary, everyday matters. He thought he was acting maturely in not judging any of the participants in this family drama and in applying to them the well-known saying "Such is life." This wisdom was supported for a time by the restraint of the newlyweds, who wanted to spare any possibly sensitive feelings in the boy. However, it soon appeared that the new spouses were no longer capable of adhering to the plan they had worked out for their behavior. Volodya began to notice that after his stepfather touched or glanced at his mother, something in her eyes would be inflamed that he, unable to call it passion, took to be something shameful. In its intense heat, this condition also seemed near to those states of his that he tried to conceal from people around him.

He learned to easily recognize in his mother her womanly arousal, and it evoked in him every time at first a vague, and then an entirely distinct, reciprocal arousal. Finding himself repulsive, Volodya would rush to the bathroom and would sit there for a long time trying to destroy—to crush—his feelings. His mother's new marriage no longer seemed an ordinary, everyday matter, and for the first time he tried out those secrets that he knew about relations between men and women, applying them to his parents, first to his father and mother, then to his mother and stepfather.

His stepfather was a strong, cheerful, and outgoing person. Volodya, on the other hand, had inherited a melancholic disposition from his father. He shunned any kind of disturbance and avoided unfamiliar people, locking himself away when they were around. His stepfather had two favorite pastimes, soccer and public baths, and he attempted to ignite in Volodya a passion for both. With soccer he was unsuccessful, but after the third invitation, the boy agreed to go to the baths. Volodya had his own reasons. In the baths, he could examine his stepfather unhindered, compare him with other men, and try to understand why his mother would burn with desire when this person touched her.

Volodya did not enjoy the baths. So many male bodies aroused in him a feeling of nausea, but he overcame it and began secretly to observe them one after the other. He returned from time to time to his stepfather, who was clearly enjoying himself, quacking like a duck and laughing loudly while he beat himself and others with birch twigs, carried on empty idle conversations, and made ill-considered acquaintances.

He did not at all stand out among the visitors to the baths. There were people who far exceeded him in the aspect that interested

Volodya, and there were others who were far inferior. But suddenly the boy's imagination transported this naked man into his mother's bedroom, where he walked with absolutely unmistakable intentions over to the boy's mother, who was waiting for him in her bed. This was so unbearable that Volodya wanted to kick his stepfather in the stomach and in the groin so that he would double over from the pain; then he would be able to kick him in the rear, causing him to sprawl on the wet floor where Volodya would trample and stomp on him, destroying his masculinity. Volodya was instantly ashamed of his fantasy and sadistic impulse. The next time he declined to keep his stepfather company.

However, once, when his father called and suggested they go on an outing together, Volodya surprised himself by answering:

"Let's go to the public baths instead."

"The baths?" his father said, taken aback. "It's true, we've never gone; but there is such a thing as taking a bath at home."

"I'd like to. I've started to get a taste for it," Volodya said, somehow both confidently and awkwardly.

"Well, I suppose . . . if you'd like to. . . . To tell the truth, I can't abide them. So many strange, naked bodies and in such close quarters. But okay, let's go."

Volodya saw his father naked for the first time, and he was stunned. His father not only did not fall short of his stepfather, he stood out among the visitors so much that they stared at him openly and shamelessly as they snickered and winked to each other in an oddly respectful way. His father frowned and hurried his son along, wishing to be gone from there as soon as possible. Volodya called to his imagination, this time consciously, the picture of his mother's bedroom, but this time the one approaching his mother's bed was not his stepfather but his father. This picture aroused in him neither horror nor repulsion. If, in his first vision, his mother had extended her hands to the one entering her bedroom, this second vision differed from the first in that there was no electricity of desire between father and mother. The woman awaited the approaching man with reluctance and irritation. And it was this reluctance and irritation that were communicated to Volodya, and not the fury and shame that had overwhelmed the boy the previous time, which had forced him to cut short his fantasy.

Volodya ceased to understand the slightest thing about the relations between his mother and her husbands. His father's spiritual and intellectual superiority to his stepfather had always seemed indisputable to him, so that he had thought that it was a matter of a secret physical defect. Now he was certain that in this area as well his father was the more perfect. So then, what? Although he pondered the question constantly and determinedly, he found no answer. Neither did the scenes leave him that now sprang up in his imagination; they appeared again and again, changing form and developing. And they became his dreams; he no longer allowed them into consciousness. But dreams cannot be stopped—in fact, they can become more and more unruly. If in the beginning his mother would cover herself with a blanket, now the blanket would always be thrown aside; sometimes the men appeared together and both approached the bed. The only aspect that now did not change in his dreams was that at the moment of final intimacy, Volodya himself pushed everyone aside, not wakening until he had brought the matter to a conclusion.

The dreams seriously complicated relations in the family and accelerated Volodya's maturing process. He tried not to look at his mother, remembering her nighttime appearances, but he also did not look at girls. They did not interest him.

However, there was in Volodya's class a recognized beauty, at whom everyone stared, each vying with the other to win her favor. Volodya would not have paid attention to her either, had she not made it so very clear that she preferred him over all the others. Once, she sent him a note inviting him to the movies. When he received the note, Volodya blushed deeply, covered his eyes, and frowned. Then, writing on the same piece of paper, he ceremoniously replied, "I am honored."

He saw that the girl anxiously followed the passage of the paper from desk to desk, then nervously unfolded it and, with a sigh of relief, smiled. She was happy. But Volodya? It seemed that the short moment of tension in which the girl had awaited an answer passed over to him for a long stay. He became gloomier and gloomier, and he walked up to the movie theater in a black mood. She took his arm and they entered the theater. There they sat silently during the entire show, permitting themselves only to intertwine their fingers (which made Volodya think nervously that his palm was sweating).

He walked her home, and so as not to be in public view, she suggested that he step into the entryway. He did.

"Let's kiss," she muttered with trembling lips.

"Yes, let's," he responded almost inaudibly, sensing a hot wind on his face. Something was approaching that he knew about from his dreams, so he closed his eyes. At that very moment, he saw the face of his mother moving toward him. However, the feeling of someone's dry lips making contact with his lips was so different from what he had dreamed that he did not even respond to the kiss, continuing to stand with eyes closed until he heard steps. He came to and saw that the girl was going up the stairs. Turning around, she saw that Volodya was following her with his eyes. She said, "Jerk."

And she added:

"Jerk, jerk, jerk."

Hanging his head, Volodya went out into the street, thinking hard about what had happened. Did he want to experience in a waking state what he experienced in his dreams? Yes, absolutely. Did he want to kiss the girl? He wanted to very much. What, then, was the matter? He racked his brains over the question until he focused on the moment before the kiss, when he had closed his eyes and seen his mother. "Never, never close your eyes," Volodya sighed, and he stopped on the street. He was seized by someone's powerful hands.

Six boys started to beat Volodya.

"Are you going to ask her out again?" they asked him, having already beaten him badly.

"I am," Volodya spat out.

They beat him some more. Passers-by walked around the fracas, trying not to look in that direction. Volodya did not know how or when he made it home. For a week he lay in bed, his mother feeding him with a spoon. Each time she leaned over and brought her face close to his, he blushed and turned his eyes away.

On his return to school, Volodya did not tell anyone about the fight. He asked the girl whether she was planning to go to the movies again and whether she would choose him as her escort. (He had worked out the phrasing in advance.) She shrugged her little shoulders contemptuously and, with every possible bit of venom and pride, answered that she would somehow find a more interesting companion.

Volodya himself did not expect to react to such an answer with enormous relief. He smiled. The girl decided that he was mocking her and nearly burst into tears. They did not speak for the rest of their school years, although everyone knew that she continued to look at Volodya from time to time and to sigh secretly. Volodya, for his part, as good as erased the episode from his life. He had his old dreams, with the same participants.

Volodya's next date did not take place until his university years. He was not in love, but he liked the girl and he decided with her help to test what would happen if he did not close his eyes. He walked to the rendezvous telling himself over and over, "Just don't close your eyes, just don't close your eyes." In the end, he directed himself to do this at the very moment his eyelids shut and his lips moved toward those of the woman. The same thing happened, absolutely the same thing, down to the words that his classmate had yelled at him the previous time. And the same events recurred later with other young women, who without fail would walk away from Volodya angered and puzzled. Not one of them questioned him about it or felt sorry for him.

Volodya stopped experimenting and began to read avidly. He was gripped by the writings of Freud, which he devoured, book after book. Even before he knew about Freud, he at some point had stumbled on the expression "Oedipus complex," and a shiver had run through him. Without understanding the meaning of the words, he sensed immediately that here possibly lurked the solution to the riddle or even the cure for his torment. Leafing through Freud, he would enter into a feverish state; he applied everything to himself, and everything fit. It even seemed to him that his case illustrated psychoanalytic theory more clearly than the patients written about in the books. The only thing that Volodya did not understand was where to find the promised deliverance. According to Freud, it was necessary to bring to consciousness everything that was stuck in the unconscious, and by itself that led to a cure. But Volodya, although still a child, as it were, was fully aware of the causes and sources of his ailment, and this did not make his life the slightest bit easier. In the foreword to the Russian translation of one of Freud's works, Professor T. Veisberg had written confidently and enthusiastically, "Thanks to psychoanalysis, which reveals bio-psycho-social strata, the inhibited and distorted emotions of neurotics are freed up and transformed into socially creative energy capable of being useful in the coming struggle for a new, communist world."

Reading this, Volodya burst out laughing and would later frequently remember these words, adding, "Well done, Professor Veisberg!" Volodya took part in the "struggle for a new, communist world"—he volunteered for communal Saturday labor and he worked in construction brigades. "Socially creative energy" he had, but his "inhibited and distorted emotions" were not cleared up in the slight-est degree, regardless of the "bio-psycho-social strata" that were revealed.

Volodya paid particular attention to Freud's interpretation of the relationship to the mother-in-law. It turned out that an aging woman, her emotional life in decline, involuntarily enters into her daughter's feelings, going so far as to fall in love with the beloved husband of her daughter. Often the hostile, sadistic components of the love impulse are directed toward the son-in-law, so as to sup-press the forbidden, tender ones all the more reliably. Such an ex-planation of the relationship as seen from the mother-in-law's side appeared quite plausible to Volodya, and he began to try to discover the reality of the relationship as seen from the other side.

The impulses of the son-in-law are similar to those just described, but they issue from a different source. According to Freud, the choice of love-object is made by a man based on the image of his mother. The beloved woman frees him from the fear of incest, for she is not a blood relative, but in a sense she does possess traits of the mother. In any event, she is chosen in the mother's own image. However, the actual place of the mother is now occupied by the mother-in-law. Freud writes, "The tendency increases to return to the choice of one's earliest days, but everything in him resists this. . . . The mother-in-law truly represents an incestuous temptation for the son-in-law. Similarly, it happens not infrequently that a man first openly falls in love with his future mother-in-law before his affections are transferred to her daughter."

This interpretation gave Volodya a certain hope. He began to think that perhaps somewhere here lay his path to recovery. To commit adultery in his heart with his mother-in-law. What hap-piness! What could be more virtuous and healthier than that? Not one's mother, but one's mother-in-law! To fall in love with his mother-in-law—this all but became Volodya's watchword when, in a state of sweet languor, he would imagine his future family life. In his opinion, this could only become a reality by traversing the stage of love for an older woman.

Meanwhile, Volodya's relationship with his mother and step-father was becoming more and more tense. So he sighed with relief when his father, upon going abroad, suggested that he move into the empty apartment, which would now belong to him (his father intended to buy a new apartment for hard currency). Volodya began to live alone, and it suited him. He worked hard and took a position in a research institute, where he became the student of Anna Aleksandrovna, a well-known scholar and a nice, warm-hearted woman.

For a time, Volodya continued his Freudian research. He gazed searchingly into the faces of older women (he began, by the way, with Anna Aleksandrovna, although she had neither daughter nor children of any kind), and he wrangled invitations to his women friends in order to see their mothers. He liked many of them, but not once did desire stir within him, not once did he "commit adultery in his heart." Soon Volodya realized that he was on the wrong track. He was even inclined to cast down the idol he had been worshiping, Freud. At any event, psychoanalytic interpretations began to irritate him. He frowned and called it all raving nonsense.

Volodya decided that it was time for him to marry. The idea of marriage took hold of him so completely that he hardly noticed what was happening around him. In the institute where he worked, a squabble was under way. Anna Aleksandrovna had quarreled with Irina Mikhailovna, a co-worker in the department and, according to general opinion, an attractive, stupid, and debauched woman. Wrapped up in his inner life, Volodya did not take the slightest part in the quarrel, although everyone expected that he would declare himself on the side of Anna Aleksandrovna. Then Anna Aleksandrovna unexpectedly passed away, and rumor pronounced

Irina Mikhailovna responsible for her death. Volodya did not go to the funeral; he only learned of it belatedly. But people told him that the impudence of Irina Mikhailovna had reached the point of her deciding to give a speech by the casket, in which, choking back her tears, she called the deceased "our conscience." Volodya received all of these stories and accounts with a coldness that shocked everyone but that was interpreted by sensitive people as "numbness." Volodya did not then suspect the role that all of these events were to play in his life. He was busy. He was thinking about marriage.

One day, while walking in the city, Volodya spotted a young woman with a simple but good-natured face. Although he had never before tried to make an acquaintance on the street, he felt a sort of inner shove and went up to her, saying (impromptu):

"Did they tell you that I was looking for you?"

"No," she said with surprise.

"They really didn't tell you?"

"Absolutely not!"

"And you don't know my telephone number?"

"I don't."

"Then write it down."

She took out her address book and looked at him questioningly, as if trying to remember under which letter to write. Volodya gave her his name, she wrote it down, and then she asked diffidently:

"What is it about?"

"You see, the fact is that I don't know your phone number. I don't even know your name, and now that I've found you, if you don't call me, we will lose each other again. You see, don't you, that we were fated to meet."

She did not immediately understand these wild words, but when his meaning sank in, she loudly burst out laughing. She told him her name was Natasha, gave him her telephone number, and agreed to go to the theater in the near future.

When they left the theater, Natasha was excited. She had enjoyed the performance, and she talked about the conception of time and about the successful treatment of the theme of baseness. She remembered Shakespeare's Sonnet 66 as well as the first line of Pasternak's poem "Hamlet." Volodya was silent and cold. Then he looked at her and saw something that always moved him, even when he wandered the streets alone and happened to glance into a woman's face, lit up by the evening street lamps: a woman's eyes with dilated pupils. Those dark depths, as it were, exuded a mystery, the solution to which was inaccessible and tantalizing. It was femininity itself. In this he sensed a certain cosmic abyss, related to those that he often discovered reading Shakespeare, or better, that Shakespeare revealed to him, not frightening him, not pushing him into it, but simply pointing out that here is an abyss. The bottomless mystery, or what amounts to the same thing, the mysterious abyss—femininity—usually intimidated Volodya, but now, supported by Shakespeare, he suddenly stopped being afraid and began passionately to speak:

"It takes great audacity to stage *Hamlet*. But no one has this audacity—only impudence combined with cowardice. In the course of a year, the director reads a few of the million volumes written about *Hamlet*. From them he learns of a thousand possible interpretations, that Hamlet lacks character, or, on the contrary, that he has an iron will, or that, possessing no clearly defined traits, he becomes each time the person his interpreter wants to present to us—whether actor, director, or commentator. Thereupon, the director, trying to retain his reading in his head, begins to realize "his vision," about which he talks in a trembling voice on the eve of the premiere. This "vision" consists, for example, in having not a young actor play Hamlet, but a fat, old one (for as you recall, "He is fat and sighs"), or in considering the role no longer appropriate for Smoktunovsky or for Gielgud, but rather for Leonov or Kramarov, or in dressing Hamlet in tails or in nothing at all, or in having him in a pit the entire time, and so forth.

These days, it also turns out that Hamlet is a regular guy, our contemporary, plays the guitar, and has progressive views although he has not joined the Young Communist League. And for historical perspective and philosophical depth, a certain 'mythos' is introduced, which superficial theater critics, not knowing the term, call symbolism and criticize for its complexity and modernism.

"But Hamlet . . . ," Volodya hesitated, "I will tell you what this tragedy is about. . . . He passionately, ecstatically, agonizingly loves his mother. His tragedy is the tragedy of his relationship with Gertrude. Everything else is a supporting voice, an overtone, the keys on a flute fingered by an unskilled hand. Hamlet barely endured his father's presence next to his mother, though he granted that, besides himself, his father was the only worthy partner for Gertrude. His father dies and Hamlet, his heart standing still, rushes to Elsinore. Now only he and he alone may and ought to be next to his mother; only he has the right to her. He puts on mourning and jealously watches Gertrude—more jealously than befits a son. He suspects something, notices something, even at the funeral, and then—'Oh, my prophetic soul'—before he could wear out the shoes he wore to the funeral, his mother gets married again, without asking Hamlet—and to whom? To the brother of her first husband, as similar to him as night is to day. To whom? To 'a nonentity,' 'a freak,' 'a lascivious scoundrel,' 'a despicable coward,' 'a usurper,' 'a fool,' and so on. All of Hamlet's rights, all of his audacious and sweet hopes to be close to his mother and perhaps even to possess her are crushed in an instant. (Isn't this the origin of his interest in 'unworn shoes,' that they have struck him in the face and in the groin?)

"And what sort of ghost is that? Who besides Hamlet hears it speak? Who can vouch that Hamlet truthfully reports its words? That Hamlet is tormented by ghosts is clear—he is giving himself over (as he had done before) to forbidden incestuous dreams about his mother. But whereas earlier, while his father was alive, he had suppressed these dreams as he went from country to country, from university to university, now his father's death (how important and how lucky that Hamlet is not its cause) unshackles the secret thoughts of the prince, although it does not free him from conscience or from consciousness of the moral law. The latter begins to find embodiment in the figure of the father's shade. Claudius is nothing; he is not an obstacle. The obstacle was his father. Now it is his shade.

"Ophelia. Beautiful, stupid, inexperienced Ophelia. She takes Hamlet's open mockery and erotic games for love. The prince uses Ophelia as a diversion and as a stimulus to provoke jealousy in Gertrude: 'Come hither, my dear Hamlet, sit by me.' 'O no, good mother, here's metal more attractive,' and with an insulting, almost obscene joke, he lies at Ophelia's feet. 'Doubt thou the stars have fire, Doubt that the sun doth move, Doubt truth to be a liar, But never doubt I love.' 'In her excellent, white bosom.' 'Came this from Hamlet to her?' Gertrude asks in surprise. She cannot believe in the sincerity of feelings expressed in such tired, banal rhymes, in such vulgarities and truisms. She knows Hamlet's real poetry and knows his temperament and the strength of his passion.

"In killing Polonius Hamlet does not for a second recall the kinship of the deceased with his erstwhile lover. In the scene with Laertes at Ophelia's grave (in front of Gertrude's eyes), the prince lets it slip: 'I loved her as forty thousand *brothers*. . . .' Brotherly love is the love of a brother—whether it is one or forty thousand. His love for Gertrude is a different matter altogether. It is not filial love. It is Hamlet's passion, and only his.

"I said that Claudius is not an obstacle for Hamlet, and that is right. The plot and the circumstances give him the opportunity many times to dispatch Claudius. And it's quite clear that he could do this with extraordinary ease, without even seeking a pretext and without fearing the consequences. But Hamlet draws out the quarrel, coming up with convincing (or not very) pretexts: either the evidence, you see, is not conclusive, or he does not want to send the black-guard to heaven (he is, after all, praying). At one point, the prince docs nevertheless attempt to murder his uncle, his mother's husband, yet this happens not just anywhere, but *in the queen's bedroom*. Accidentally getting in the way, the fumbling Polonius dies, about whom the casual joke is made that he is at a banquet not where he is eating but where he is eaten. But why in the world does Hamlet delay Claudius' 'punishment'? Because before killing him, Hamlet has to enjoy his triumph. He has to reveal to Gertrude his uncle's complete insignificance. He has to ensure that the queen sees her husband as weak and pitiful. She must of her own free will repudiate her husband and choose Hamlet herself.

"The performance that Hamlet arranges is primitive and crude, but it is calculated quite precisely. Only a dimwit would not understand what the play given for Claudius was hinting at, and only a man with the iron nerves of a murderer could take that hint without becoming agitated (as Claudius, by the way, cannot). Claudius is, in point of fact, weaker than Hamlet. Understanding that he has received a virtually undisguised challenge, Claudius leaves the arena in fear before it can become a field of battle. Hamlet triumphs. Gertrude has seen. And he is rewarded, oh, how he is rewarded. The queen sends for him. She will receive him *in her bedchamber*.

"So he flies to her. He flies feeling himself hero and victor. He is near his goal. He plays using his muscles. He plays with Rosenkranz and Guildenstern, explaining to them along the way that they may not play with him—not because it is wrong to play with a person but because no one is capable of playing with him, Hamlet, the philosopher, the athlete, and the victor over Claudius.

"He arrives in her bedchamber in full fighting trim and fully armed. It is his shining hour. At first, he speaks insinuatingly of the good qualities of his father, Gertrude's first husband, contrasting them with the miserable flaws of his uncle, his mother's second husband. Then, with great subtlety, he speaks of the 'incestuous bed,' describing in detail his uncle's lascivious joy and vileness. And how many times had his powerful imagination tormented him with these scenes. But, after all, he is speaking of his mother's bed. And where does that little word 'incest' come from? Think about it. Which relationship is Hamlet talking about? No one in any period has ever considered a union such as Gertrude's second marriage incestuous. That word pops up out of the prince's darkest and most secret depths and is extraordinarily relevant to his goals. It is not only that he speaks in haste and lets slip his secret desire. He also makes clear that a relationship with him should not be frightening, that incest has *already* been committed and committed with a pitiful and unworthy person and that the mistake can only be corrected by choosing a love object that is different and more appropriate in every way. The queen is confused. Hamlet in her eyes possesses shattering strength. She wilts and falls weakly into his arms. And there it is; it has happened. But Hamlet is not as strong as his poor mother thinks, nor as decisive as he himself thinks. At the very apogee of his triumph, his tormentor appears, his jailor and executioner, who is nothing but a ghost, albeit a ghost that no one can see or hear besides Hamlet. But this ghost is Hamlet's father, the lawful husband of the queen. It is he who stops Hamlet. The moment is lost. Embarrassed and even a bit disappointed, Gertrude asks what she should do now. Her son with bitterness and spite advises her to return to the embraces of his uncle, to take pleasure in his pinches and his little games, and to forget everything that was—and might have been—between her and Hamlet.

"From this moment on, Hamlet does not pose the question 'to be or not to be.' He is still living on his own momentum and, by force of habit, he even sometimes takes action, but he is doomed. He now really wishes the death of Claudius and looks for a pretext for his murder. He is calm in the face of intrigues, and he coldbloodedly turns them against Rosenkranz and Guildenstern. He knows how to play their stops. In accepting his fate, he emerges dignified and ready for death. However, he is sure that Claudius will die first. He does not wish the death of his mother, but he observes it almost with aloofness. It is now merely the necessary pretext for the execution of Claudius. The only thing that concerns him is that no one ever find out the true meaning of his story. For that reason he asks Horatio, who is in on everything, to recount of his life only the external outline of events, concealing what is most important. 'The rest is silence,' he warns his friend, placing a finger to his dying lips."

Volodya fell silent, but the energy of his narrative had not yet died down within him, and it traveled through his body in waves. He looked at his companion. She maintained a spellbound silence. Then, smiling weakly, she said, "Unhappy prince," and added, nearly inaudibly, as if to herself, "Poor Ophelia." Volodya pulled her toward him, threw his arms around her, and, with eyes closed, kissed first one cheek, then the other, then her neck, without being able to find her lips. Understanding instantly that he did not know how to kiss, and surprised at the incongruity of that fact with Volodya's apparent experience and his susceptibility to passion, she caught his lips, carefully ran her tongue over them, opened them, prying them one from the other, and held the kiss an astoundingly long time. She did not give Volodya an opportunity to pause. She was aroused not so much by the actions of a man she liked as by the happiness of Diotima, giving instructions in love to the awkward wise man. She brought both herself and her stunned partner nearly to the point of breathlessness and to the point of losing both a sense of reality and consciousness.

They then stood a long time, exhausted by their kiss, which to all appearances for both of them was going to be, or perhaps was already, a unique "rite de passage." Like every transitional rite, it had no temporal extension. It was an eruption in which an entire epoch burst into being, took form, and died away. It was as God said, in the words of the theologians: "One day is as a thousand years; a thousand years are as one day." The kiss also left in Volodya a feeling of nearly total emptiness. With this feeling, he parted from Natasha, saying goodbye in the entryway.

As he made his way home, the emptiness in his soul began to be penetrated, nearly inaudibly at first, by a fanfare of rejoicing, which, for some reason, gave rise to a nervous irritability. Volodya lamented his lack of skill and Natasha's evident experience. But more than anything, he was angry at the inappropriateness of his own extemporized speech on Hamlet and even more at the fact that it seemed to him that he had not thought up all of that himself but had possibly read it at some point in some Freudian book or other. And what had Natasha understood? "Poor Ophelia." Volodya remembered her words with indignation and shrugged his shoulders: "What has Ophelia got to do with anything?" However, thinking it over, he found these words to be not quite so foolish, and Ophelia even seemed quite deeply involved with the dramatic situation, the tragedy, the plot, and also with the hero. In his thoughts, Volodya returned to Natasha and began—already with delight—to resurrect in his memory every subtle nuance of that incommensurable kiss. It had been so rich in events that it could have been compared to the history of an entire people. Volodya set about reexperiencing its taste, its color, its smell, and its sound. Soon artists, poets, and musicians came to the aid of the historian, but they were in the end ousted by the novelist.

By the time the latter had appeared, Volodya, with the help of the historian, had already reconstructed the episode during the kiss when one of its participants closed his eyes. The researcher knew full well what had happened in analogous episodes with the same historical character. This time history did not repeat itself! This was so significant that the episode became virtually central to the entire story. Volodya was even somewhat reluctant to leave the learned historian so as to devote his attention to the quite inexperienced novelist.

The novelist persuaded the hero that it was necessary, in the end, to make some sort of decision. So after pondering for a minute over a blank piece of paper, Volodya wrote words that he had composed earlier when he had been weighing and experimenting with different versions. Now he had only to choose one of the versions already spinning in his head. At the top of the paper he wrote, "Natasha," placing a comma after it (a comma and not an exclamation mark). Then without filling the page with anything else, in the lower right corner, he signed his name: "Volodya."

Below the signature there was still some space, so Volodya wrote in small letters, "PS," writing a single line on this side of the page and transferring the remaining portion of the postscript to the next page. In a clear hand, Volodya wrote:

"I wanted the unfilled space not so much to divide our names as to draw them together. I did not have the courage to write them right next to each other, but I did dare to make this audacious experiment in my thoughts, and . . . and, I succeeded. Natasha!

Volodya

PPS. That's how!

Reading the letter over, Volodya found it pompous. He always found words pompous that he composed to express his feelings, but after being praised by the addressee he would begin to consider them successful. For this reason, the feeling of pomposity nearly always coincided with the pleasurable anticipation of success. Perhaps, indeed, these were not two different feelings but the same one, highly nuanced.

After sending the letter, he became nervous. The answer, according to his present way of thinking, might not be what he was counting on. When he finally opened the envelope addressed by Natasha, his hands were shaking. The letter read:

My dear, my dear, my dear!

Your Natasha

Volodya smiled and wiped the perspiration from his brow. Everything was going as it should. That very day, he phoned Natasha saying that he had something extremely important to tell her and asked permission to stop by her apartment that evening. Natasha lived with her mother, and Volodya realized, albeit not immediately, that he wanted to speak with Natasha not on the street or at any other location, but in her apartment in order to have the opportunity for a look at her mother.

On his arrival, Volodya handed the bouquet of flowers to the older of the two ladies, and she received them unaffectedly and graciously. She had the same open, friendly face as Natasha. She and Volodya immediately liked each other, they spoke in a confiding tone, and they exchanged amiable, understanding smiles. The whole time they were drinking tea and talking, Volodya was trying to fathom whether an erotic component was mixed in the sympathy he instantly felt toward the lady of the house. But his search was fruitless, and, in a cheerful mood, as always when Freud's theory seemed to misfire, he said to himself, "Well done, Professor Veisberg!"

When the evening was nearing its end and it was time for the guest to be taking his leave, Volodya, as if remembering something, addressed Natasha's mother with the words:

"Actually, as a matter of fact, I came to ask you for your daughter's hand. . . ."

There was not the slightest awkwardness. The women simply looked at each other and burst out laughing as one. The future mother-in-law answered without hesitation:

"She is yours, Volodya." And she kissed him on the forehead.

By the wish of the groom, the wedding was to be extremely traditional. While the preparations went ahead, the bride continued to live with her mother, although both women were prepared for Natasha to move at once into the apartment of her future husband. Volodya, for his part, undertook renovations and repeatedly rearranged the furniture. While awaiting the appointed time, he visited Natasha in her apartment every day, visibly enjoying his conversations with his mother-in-law. Then there occurred the meeting of the parents, and Volodya attentively compared his mother and mother-in-law as they sat next to each other. It was clear that they were not alike in anything and that either Freud was always deceiving Volodya (and humanity), or Volodya was now pulling the wool over his (Freud's) eyes, because, without the slightest doubt, his marriage choice had not been based on his mother.

"Victory," Volodya rejoiced, "This is victory."

He was so tired during that period that he immediately fell asleep as soon as he lay down in the evening, and no dreams came to him.

"That's the end of it," Volodya decided, and was happy.

At their wedding, Natasha and Volodya drank a lot and barely made it to their bed. Their first night was chaste. In the morning, Volodya began to worry—as he knew, it was not the first time for Natasha. But for him, there had only been experience in dreams, which were better unremembered. Natasha, guessing his state of mind, took charge, but she overestimated her experience, and it was all over before it had begun.

Volodya was in despair and lay turned to the wall. She tenderly consoled him, saying that they still had everything to look forward to, and he decided to wait until evening in order to try once again. In the evening they undressed and lay down together, but no matter how hard he tried, desire did not awaken in his body. The flesh had died, as it were. Then he applied extreme measures: while kissing his wife, he closed his eyes. His vision, his delightful nightmare reappeared, and the flesh revived instantly. Volodya opened his eyes only when he felt that his duty had been accomplished. And that was, in fact, how he remembered his wedding night—no pleasure, only the performance of a duty.

It was the same on other nights. Volodya no longer tried to tempt fate, and he closed his eyes immediately. Of course, this was a simulacrum of intimacy with Natasha, and she could not but feel this. She did not speak about it, but their lives were joyless. Two months after the wedding, so as not to torment his wife, Volodya proposed that they separate. She at first objected, saying that everything would still turn out all right, but there was no conviction in her voice, and he stood his ground.

No one understood why this marriage, which by every indication promised to be happy, had dissolved so quickly. But the former spouses did not explain anything to anybody.

Volodya was morose for some time. Then he decided that evidently such was his fate, that his sexual life was over, but that life itself was not. There were work and friends, and he dedicated his days to labor and friendship. And he achieved success in both areas with surprising ease, showing in both a rare talent.

One evening, Volodya went to a party at the home of a friend who lived nearby. There were a lot of people there, but Volodya was surprised to find among the guests his colleague, Irina Mikhailovna. Volodya turned out to be practically the star of the evening. He talked a lot, made everyone laugh, and charmed everyone.

The guests departed long after midnight, happy with the refreshments, the conversation, and the dancing. The host asked Volodya to accompany Irina Mikhailovna home, she having come this evening without her husband. Irina Mikhailovna gaily took Volodya's arm and they went to a taxi stand. Volodya was pondering the sort of conversation to engage his companion with, when she suddenly burst out laughing and explained ingenuously, "I want something to eat."

"That is because," Volodya said, almost seriously, "you didn't drink much. Otherwise you would have had to nibble on something."

"Volodenka, is there anything to drink at your place? Don't you live somewhere around here?"

Concealing his surprise, Volodya answered carelessly:

"Yes, it seems to me I have vodka . . . and sausage. . . ."

"Let's go, let's go, Volodenka, my dear," and Irina Mikhailovna clapped her hands.

Volodya looked at her with interest, and making a gesture of invitation, he turned toward his home.

"What a nice place you have, and so many books," Irina Mikhailovna said on entering. "Why didn't you ever invite me over before? I would have come with pleasure. I have always had warm feelings for you. Did you know that? But what a question. You knew, of course you knew. So shall we have a drink? What shall we drink to? Let's drink to this evening. It was wonderful. Oh, that's good. Let's have another. Volodenka, come on, pour us another. But why are you so silent? You were so cheerful the whole evening. Yes, yes, I know what that cheerfulness cost you, I understand, my dear, I understand. . . ."

Volodya stood up and leaned against the wall. His head was spinning. No woman had ever spoken to him that way before. She stood up as well and, moving almost up against him, placed her left hand on his chest.

"I will help you, my darling," she said. "I will help. My poor unhappy dear," she muttered almost inaudibly. Her hand, thrust into the interval between the buttons of his shirt, was stroking his chest, and her sharp, manicured, red fingernails now and then scratched his skin, lightly but penetratingly.

Volodya stood without moving, nearly aloof, with eyes closed, thinking over the oddness of the scene in which the man and the woman seemed to have swapped roles. To him had fallen the role of the old virgin, coldly yielding to insistent importunities only because, at some point or other, this, too, was something people had to go through. As far as Irina Mikhailovna was concerned, she performed her seducer's role flawlessly and in accordance with the classical rules. The shirt Volodya was wearing became unbuttoned, and the lines "breast under kisses, like under flowing water" went through his head as he observed the events from the side.

Soon he found himself on his bed, undressed and lying on his back while above him floated the luminously tender face of Irina Mikhailovna. He felt the weight of her body and occasionally made out her words.

"Darling, dearest, I will save you, yes, I will. Don't tremble so, everything will be fine, you'll see."

She took his hands and moved them over her body, occasionally halting the motion and pressing them to those delightful places so coveted by men. Volodya's passivity was not limitless. He could not fail to participate at the minimal level required of him in his position. Everything confirmed his long-held conviction that in relations between the sexes, the woman is the one who takes and the man the one who gives, although, by way of compensation, the actual activity is preceded by a sham game with a carefully worked-out system of rules, prohibitions, and ceremonies, in which the woman symbolically gives herself to her supposed conqueror.

This train of thought suddenly broke off but found its confirmation in the fact that a moment later he lay completely exhausted and empty. At that moment, he viewed himself once again from the side and simultaneously not so much heard as felt an agonizing sound emanating from his throat but not seeming to belong to him. Volodya was sobbing—bitterly, unrestrainedly. Tears poured down hot, as in childhood, and Volodya understood that, in truth, he had not given himself over entirely to women, but that he was now giving himself over—to weeping.

Irina lay on the pillow next to him, placed his head on her shoulder, and gently, silently stroked him, from time to time wiping away his tears and glancing into his eyes. She understood what was happening with Volodya. She thought that perhaps it was precisely this outcome she had been trying to achieve. Together with his tears, the heavy feeling deserted Volodya. His eyes were still blinded and unfocused, but he was already no longer moaning, nor was he shivering or gnashing his teeth.

Quite suddenly, and without any transition, Volodya felt like the hero of the fairy tale who had jumped from the third and final cauldron with boiling milk and had emerged young and energetic. At the same instant, his eyes recovered their sight, and this recovery of sight was incomparably more unbelievable than jumping out of a cauldron, because level with his eyes a few centimeters from them lived and breathed the most perfect of creations with a delicate, pink bud (the other of which served as a pillow for Volodya's cheek). A divine lightness, having lodged in Volodya and filled him with inexpressible rapture, lifted him upward in an instant, and neither of them noticed how or when Volodya caught in his lips that most delicate of nipples, which had restored his sight to him and which now had become hard and tense in answer to the movements of his tongue and lips. His joy turned into a triumphant, victorious feeling. He forgot who, in his opinion, was supposed to take and who to give. He forgot about everything and obeyed the wonderful rhythm that was now undoubtedly governing the entire world and not just his tiny (so light and joyous) part of it.

"Oh," said Irina, smiling encouragingly.

"Oh?" she said, surprised.

"Oh!" she said, pleased.

"Oh . . ." she said, faintly.

"Oh . . . ooh . . . oooh!" she moaned and shrieked.

"Oooooh!!" she cried out with sharp, excruciating pleasure. Tears were now flowing down her face.

Volodya kissed her eyes and gazed back at all of her, worshiping her body and filled with gratitude, even reverence, because—and he knew this with certainty—a miracle had occurred. He had been a witness to and a participant in it. He had lived within that wondrous rhythm that has no temporal dimension and without knowledge of which one can consider one's life wasted. For the happiness of his new knowledge, Volodya was entirely indebted to Irina.

Both were silent. Volodya began to think about that blessed condition in which they now existed and that is called tristia post coitum. He had earlier supposed that this tristia was familiar to him, but now it was clear that the present luminous, light tristia had nothing in common with his usual sadness, which would only become intensified post coitum.

Soon Volodya sank into a deep sleep. On awakening, he immediately reached out his hand for Irina. But she was not there. Volodya did not want to believe it, literally searching his apartment, looking behind the door-curtains and even under the bed. Then he noticed on the night table a volume of Pushkin with a bookmark. Thinking that a note had been placed inside the book, Volodya opened it, but there was no note. However, in the text the following words had been marked off: "He, a handsome man, imagined himself hideous and avoided the company of people unfamiliar to him, intimidated by their mocking glances."

Volodya gave a start. Apparently, the marked-off words had been intended as a note. Despite his agitation, Volodya sat down at the table and thought hard about it. What did Irina want to say? He had formerly not considered her at all intelligent, but behind the quotation-cum-message he sensed a woman's penetrating insight and an extremely subtle intuition. The words she had chosen from the Pushkin text became for their new addressee not merely a message but an extraordinary event.

Volodya knew these words well, not having missed them when he read Pushkin's remarks "On Byron and Other Important Subjects." Now he reread the piece carefully and was struck by how much space was devoted to "Lord Byron's peculiarities," and even more by the fact that nearly a third of the article consisted of diary excerpts, in which the "8-year-old Byron" described his love life: "at an age when I not only could not experience passion, I did not understand the meaning of the word. And yet it was passion!" "At that time," it said in the diary, "and for some years after, I had no notion of the difference between the sexes. Nevertheless, my suffering, my love for this little girl was so strong that I sometimes find myself doubting whether I have ever really loved since then."

The list of the lord's peculiarities ends with the sentence marked off by Irina: "He, a handsome man, imagined himself hideous. . . ." Volodya's skin went cold: Could Irina have understood *everything* about him? Could his miraculous recovery have been a *conscious* treatment? He remembered her promise to save him. An awful thought flickered in Volodya, as if some rude, unpleasant person explained in a haughty voice that there had been no miracle but merely a trick that is easy to perform.

And another thought transfixed Volodya: Could the entire course of his current thoughts have been guessed in advance by Irina, or even prescribed by her? She had explained, "You are not hideous, it is not true. You are handsome." But would this mean then that there had been no metamorphosis, no transformation of monster into prince, in other words, no love to have generated the transformation? In that case, what had there been?

Volodya remembered the happiness that he felt from the previous day's state of mind, which, in his experience of it, had had no temporal dimension. Then, with a shudder, he suddenly reflected that women often determine with nearly mathematical precision the duration of coitus. "This one," they say contemptuously, "is incapable of more than five minutes, but that one is superb." Volodya plunged into feverish calculations but was unable to arrive at any conclusion and so remained with the horrifying suspicion that Irina for her part had calculated the whole thing and had been dissatisfied with the brevity of what to her partner had seemed limitless and immeasurable in duration.

These thoughts tormented Volodya as much as the feeling of physical loss due to Irina's departure. It turned out that he did not know her address, or even her telephone number, which he at one point had written down on a piece of paper that he had then lost. This had not bothered him because he had never supposed he would need her number.

Volodya began to do foolish things. He called nearly all of his fellow workers trying to get hold of Irina's telephone number. Each time he offered some absurd excuse for needing it. His fellow workers showed interest, questioned him about details, but did not have her number. What with the general enmity toward Irina, no one maintained a relationship with her. Finally, Volodya had the sense to call the apartment where he had been the evening before. After thanking his host for a wonderful evening, he said that he wanted to inquire as to whether Irina Mikhailovna reached home safely but that he had lost her telephone number somewhere. . . .

One minute later Volodya was again dialing the telephone and with a wildly beating heart heard it ring.

"Irina Mikhailovna?"

"Yes, Volodya my dear," she said, recognizing his voice immediately. "How nice of you to call. Thank you for seeing me home last night. I haven't stayed out so late for a long time. When I arrived, my husband was already very worried. By the way, he says hello."

"Irina, I want to see you," Volodya said, stammering and some-how strangely tongue-tied.

"Yes, of course, I'll be at work tomorrow."

"No, I don't mean at work."

"Yes, I remember, we have a staff meeting. I hope it won't drag on. My husband and I are going to the theater."

"Irina. . . ."

"Yes, my dear. Is something wrong?"

"Damn it! I don't know how to carry on this sort of conversation!" Volodya cursed.

"You know, I am very glad that we were able to have such a good talk yesterday. I always knew that we would work everything out and that you wouldn't be able to take part in the witch-hunt. All the more since I'm not a monster, right?"

"Irina, what are you saying?"

"You know what? Come visit us. Let me ask Sergei Ivanovich. Wait just a second. Seryozhenka, I am inviting Volodya to come see us. When? On Saturday? Fine. On Saturday, Volodenka, is that all right? Do come! Sergei Ivanovich has wanted to meet you for a long time. He has read all of your articles and is very impressed. So you'll come?"

"It's a whole week until Saturday!"

"So, fine, it's arranged. See you tomorrow. Good-bye!"

"Bye!"

"Damn it! Idiotic conversation!" Volodya raged, throwing down the receiver.

The next day he arrived early at the institute and wandered the corridors, noticed by everyone. Irina, on the other hand, was late even for the beginning of the meeting. As she always did, she passed through the room with a challenging air about her, settling in an unoccupied seat which, alas, was not next to Volodya's. The meeting was exceptionally detailed and slow. Volodya twisted and turned in his seat. His whole body was hot, his hands shook, and he was unable to concentrate on a single thought. Luckily, his participation in the meeting was limited to his mere presence, but his nervousness was noticed by nearly everyone. As soon as the talking stopped, Volodya jumped up and pushed his way through to Irina in three bounds.

"Irina Mikhailovna," he said. "Would you be able to give me a couple of minutes? I have a few questions for you."

"Yes, yes, of course, Volodya. Let's talk."

They went along the corridor to the stairwell, where people could smoke and talk almost without hindrance. They were followed by astonished looks. Those colleagues whom Volodya had asked for Irina's telephone number at once connected the previous day's call with today's encounter and instantly shared their inferences with each other. Volodya did not know what he wanted to say or where to begin. She also was silent, and for a minute they just smoked, without speaking.

"So, my dear?" she finally uttered.

"I . . . love you," he said with difficulty.

"No, my dear." She smiled.

"Don't you dare, don't you dare talk that way!" he demanded.

"It's the truth," she said gently.

"And . . . you?" he choked.

"Darling, my dearest, I like you very much. What happened between us made me happy, and I will never forget it. Of all the men I have met, you are the best, but in fact I took advantage of your temporary blindness. You didn't take a good look at me. Look more closely. I am fifteen years older than you, an old woman, well, almost an old woman. Don't think about me. Love other women. Love many others. You are wonderful, smart, and good; every woman will fall in love with you. Only don't be afraid of the likes of us girls. And if you can't not think about the Eternal Feminine, then write poetry, because a girl is a girl—something altogether different."

Stunned by this wild talk, Volodya nevertheless admitted into consciousness an irritated observation regarding the last phrase about "poetry and girls": "What a collection of cheap clichés!" He had the urge to offend Irina with the pointed question (but one that greatly agitated him): "How many minutes did our session last?" But he restrained himself, or lacked the courage to say this. He simply asked:

"When are you going to come over?"

"Come see us, Volodenka. I will introduce you to Sergei; I'm sure you will hit it off. We will have the ceremonial toast to our friendship, do you want to? Then we will use "ty" even on the telephone."[1]

"I want you to come over."

"Well, all right," Irina said, indicating with her eyes newly arrived smokers. "We will talk about this again. What you have told me is very interesting, but I cannot really answer your questions right now. I have to clarify something for myself. And so now, forgive me, I have to go. We're off to the theater tonight."

Rumors of Volodya's affair shook the entire institute.

"It was to be expected," some said. "From the fact alone of how he behaved when Anna Aleksandrovna died, it was clear that he would betray her memory."

"It's monstrous," others said. "The beloved student of Anna Aleksandrovna unites with the murderer of his teacher. It's simply impossible to believe."

"Just think," said still others. "She is, you know, twenty years older than he, if not more. Even for her extensive practice, that's something new."

People began to talk about the "shocking affair." Those who were benevolently inclined took Volodya aside and warned him. They

---

1. *Translator's note*: In traditional Russian culture, people who have been using formal address with each other, "vy," make the transition to using informal address, "ty," by drinking a ceremonial toast, with linked arms, followed by a kiss.

recounted savory tidbits from Irina's biography; they piously remembered Anna Aleksandrovna, who had been like a mother to him, more than a mother. They gave him advice. Volodya did not even get angry. He simply did not listen to all this balderdash. Nevertheless, the words "Anna Aleksandrovna, like a mother" for some reason stuck in his brain and became a sort of grotesque background for his unconnected thoughts about Irina.

"Irina," he said, as one possessed, "Irina." And he saw her, naked, lying in his bed, or sitting astride himself or swallowing tears of pleasure or wiping the tears from his cheeks. "Irina," he whispered. "Like a mother . . . Anna Aleksandrovna . . . like a mother . . . what am I saying? . . . What nonsense!"

But it was not nonsense, and Volodya soon understood this. Anna Aleksandrovna, in fact, had often manifested toward Volodya a tenderness that she was pleased to think maternal, although evil tongues (the same ones that now spoke of parental feelings) hinted at a different source of the relations between the elderly woman and the young student. Volodya had never before wished to delve into the reasons—real or imaginary—for his good relationship with her. He considered that with Anna Aleksandrovna he had enjoyed a professional relationship strengthened by mutual good-will and honesty. He may have owed her nothing as his teacher, but she always liked to call him her student, and she was openly proud of him. Without any ulterior considerations, he took on himself the assigned role, which, nevertheless, was hardly a burden. Volodya knew how to appreciate good-will and he knew how to be grateful. Seen from the side, Volodya and Anna Aleksandrovna were a touching sight: the respected, talented student and the maternally tender, and just as maternally proud, teacher. It is impossible to deny that there was sufficient foundation for such a view. The more Volodya thought about this, the stronger his desire now became to persuade himself that that was the way it had been.

Over several years, Volodya had observed the course of relations between Irina and Anna Aleksandrovna. At the beginning, Anna Aleksandrovna gently but ever so insistently offered her tutelage to Irina, but the latter for some reason cherished her independence and firmly refused the honor. Despite this, Anna Aleksandrovna maintained a friendly tone and demonstratively—perhaps even excessively demonstratively—refused to listen to rumors about Irina's escapades (about which, nevertheless, she was well informed). Irina, for her part, behaved indecorously and unintelligently, either by petty, impudent fault-finding at meetings, or by incautiously hurling words about in public. Finally, they quarreled, interrupting the feud only once—and not for long—when Irina went up to Anna Aleksandrovna to tell her that she considered Volodya's latest article brilliant. Later there occurred that horrible episode, after which Anna Aleksandrovna died from a heart spasm. Irina at a staff meeting had said then that Anna Aleksandrovna had presented the matter in such a way that any criticism of her would begin to seem like a witch-hunt and like the persecution of a decent, intelligent person by an ignorant and malicious mob.

"What in the world are you saying?" Anna Aleksandrovna had said, smiling, as she grabbed at her heart and, five minutes later, died.

Then came the funeral, Irina's provocative speech by the coffin, her filibustering at the institute, and so forth.

Volodya only gradually realized why he was pursuing these reflections. Irina now had total command over his thoughts and feelings. She had cured him of a lasting and grave passion for his mother, which had warped his life. Now in order to be with a woman, he did not have to conjure up the image of his mother. But Volodya was not satisfied. He also required a cure at the symbolic level. For had not Irina defeated Volodya's symbolic mother, Anna Aleksandrovna? After symbolically murdering her, Irina had conquered her heir, Volodya. Was that not a symbol? Was that not the victory of natural forces over perverse, incestuous ones? Volodya's thoughts then became completely mythological, turning—almost unpremeditatedly—into *pensée sauvage*. Volodya found a peculiar pleasure in this.

Volodya impatiently awaited Saturday, when he was to visit Irina's home. Carrying a bottle of vodka and a cake, he arrived at the designated time and was cordially received by Irina and Sergei Ivanovich. Everything was extremely warm and pleasant. Seryozha turned out to be a very nice, intelligent person. Irina poured the tea and gazed softly at Volodya. Seryozha continually but good-naturedly teased his wife. Volodya realized that he knew about her adventures but that he did not ascribe great importance to them, valuing instead the warmth and lack of constraint in their relationship.

However, the domesticity of the encounter charmed Volodya only for a short while, and he soon began to fidget nervously. He had to at least touch Irina, but he was afraid of looking up one more time, so he did not look at her, even when Sergei Ivanovich left the room. The visit gave Volodya no more pleasure than the telephone conversation. He decided to obtain an explanation from Irina at his own home, no matter what.

Irina, however, knew how to avoid explanations, and at the institute she only occasionally grazed Volodya's hand while walking past, which only increased his torment. Once while thinking disconnectedly about Irina, Volodya wrote an insane poem:

> *Give me to drink. . . . A swallow of cool liquid*
> *And an ungreedy, quiet breath of air.*
> *And I'll leave again without filling the flask,*
> *I'll leave by one of many roads.*
>
> *But you'll see that I raised to my dry lips*
> *The empty mug, its liquid spilled.*
> *I pointlessly mentioned spillage and drying up*
> *And I was surprised by my own words.*

You understand everything and you know that it's no shame
To ask for water, and you know that I am ashamed
By my too apparent thirst
And by my striving toward your springs.

Give me to drink. . . . Water. . . . One more swallow
That's all. . . . the end. . . .

Writing these lines down on paper, Volodya realized that they were crazy, and he was annoyed at their tone of hysteria. But he could not do anything about it, so he did not tear up the paper but instead carefully wrote underneath the poem the date of its composition. He almost decided to give the poem to Irina but at the last moment lost heart and hid it in the inner pocket of his jacket. He carried it about with him for a long time, thinking that perhaps he would somehow take courage and hand it to its addressee.

Soon fate brought Volodya and Irina together at the same apartment where their relationship had begun. Again there was eating, drinking, and dancing. Volodya sat across from Irina, who had again come without her husband. He hoped to leave with her and to get her to his place.

One of the guests had brought with him a person whom nobody knew and who was called Misha. He was a pilot, wore a leather jacket, had lively eyes with small pupils, and revealed gold teeth when he smiled. This person was placed next to Irina, and as he sat down he immediately in a loud voice let loose a vulgar expression in her direction. She did not frown, but, on the contrary, she burst out laughing unrestrainedly and sonorously. Volodya wanted to score against Misha and he got off several witticisms, but the subtlety of his wit was inaccessible to the man with the transparent eyes. Irina looked over at Volodya without smiling, as if she disapproved.

The dancing began and Volodya noticed that Irina danced and smooched with the pilot uninterruptedly. He left the room and began to examine books, but when he returned, he noticed that a sort of awkward feeling had come over the guests. He heard the whisper, "Irina's at it again." He began to look around for her, but he did not find her. And Misha was also missing. Volodya felt instantly cold. Guests exchanged glances and gazed at the bathroom door that, as it turned out, had been locked already for twenty minutes. Behind the door could be heard the sound of running water.

Dessert was served and still the door did not open. Only when tea was poured did a cheerful and invigorated Irina come out of the bathroom, powdering her neck and face on the way, as if nothing had happened. A minute later, amid general embarrassment, a manly Misha also emerged from the bathroom. However, one could not have called him invigorated. His vulgar joking had ceased. He had become gloomy. Misha sat in silence next to Irina, and she rained down on him a storm of lively ridicule, which could only be considered insulting. The pilot became ever gloomier and then, somehow unnoticed by all, disappeared, as if he had evaporated.

On every point on his body Volodya felt pins and needles. He shook from the piercing cold but at the same time was drenched in hot sweat. He was horrified at Irina the same way Don José had to be horrified at Carmen, but nevertheless he met the glance of her black, sparkling eyes with rapture. He strove to imagine in detail what had happened in the bathroom and he saw it distinctly. He burned and shivered.

"I'll see you home," he said.

"But I still want to stay for a while, with your kind permission, Volodenka."

She drank tea and ate pastry. She chatted about something with the host while Volodya waited for her feverishly. Finally she turned to him:

"Volodenka, will you put me in a taxi?"

"Yes, of course."

They left.

"I have a big favor to ask," Volodya said, "I feel like I'm getting sick and probably won't go to the institute tomorrow. But I absolutely have to hand in an outline of my report. Will you please stop by my place for a minute and take the outline?"

"Oh, I'd rather not, my dear. I'm very tired and it's already late. What's the matter with you?"

"Chills. I think I have a fever."

Irina placed her hand on Volodya's forehead and saw that he was not lying.

"All right, I'll dash in, but only for a second, okay?"

Volodya opened the door and let Irina go first. Flicking on the switch, in an instant he embraced Irina from behind, painfully squeezing her breasts with both hands.

"Don't," she said sharply, taking his hands away.

"Why not?"

"I don't want to."

"You don't want to? So what? I want to all the more," Volodya said, his hands traveling around her dress.

"Get away!" she said angrily, tearing herself loose.

But he held on to her. Undoing the buttons, he tore off the hooks on her dress, and his open mouth sucked on her neck. He breathed heavily, snarling from time to time. Finally, he undressed her and began to knead her body, noticing coldly and without a shred of jealousy the marks of her recent pleasures. He even kissed these marks, making them more noticeable. Irina resisted long and almost savagely. Then, evidently, something ignited within her too, and she began to yield to his onslaught. Although she still did not respond to his kisses, she pulled him to herself, as if involuntarily.

Volodya shot an unconscious look at his watch and began, in the true sense of the word, to work, putting into his labor much effort and all of his accumulated theoretical knowledge. Irina breathed quickly and loudly, more and more drawn into their joint activity. She moved voluptuously, intermittently embraced Volodya, and asked him to do something. Volodya did not hear her words but he must have understood, for he did everything she asked. Three times, Irina tried to move away, but Volodya did not allow her to, and each time she became inflamed once more and again demonstrated her ardor and skill.

Releasing Irina, Volodya glanced again at his watch. "Thirty-two minutes exactly," he muttered to himself with the intonation of a telephone recording that answers requests for the exact time.

"Many thanks," he said coldly, "I am satisfied."

She looked at him with surprise.

"Thank you, doctor," he repeated. "The treatment is completed." And to himself he thought: "Thirty-two minutes—not bad." And then he thought bitterly, "What exactly have I measured?"

Early the next morning Volodya was awakened by the telephone. Half awake, Volodya picked up the receiver, but before he managed to say "hello" he heard uncontrollable sobbing.

"What? What is this?" he cried, and he was forced to repeat his question many times before he understood that his stepfather was calling and was trying to inform him that his mother had died that night.

Volodya collapsed into a chair. His hands instantly went stony cold. He sat paralyzed for a long time, mentally lifting the dropped telephone receiver from the floor but unable to move even a finger. The first thing he was aware of, after his stepfather's communication had sunken in, was a feeling that his heart, apart from the terrible pain, was pierced by yet another idea that was related to his mother's death. What sort of idea was it? Volodya could not grasp it. But soon one word burned its way into his brain with flaming letters, expressing this idea perfectly. He read the word, his face contorting in horror: "Irina."

"Irina? Why Irina?" he asked, and he proceeded to mutter nearly unconsciously, "Irina. . . . Anna Aleksandrovna. . . . Murderer! . . . Mama! . . ."

Then again: "Irina? Why Irina?" And already firmly, distinctly, with complete clarity: "I summoned her. I brought it on myself."

His thoughts swam chaotically and unconnectedly, but Volodya quickly understood their logic and was all but crushed by it. Only recently he had thought of Irina as the woman who had committed the symbolic act of killing his "more-than-a-mother." He had reached out to her, anticipating victory over the tormenting image of his mother. However, no one aside from Volodya saw any symbolism in the death of Anna Aleksandrovna, and what sort of symbolism could one speak of after the death not of the image in Volodya's soul, but of his real, (as Volodya even put it) his live mother? Volodya knew with certainty that this actual death, following immediately the symbolic killing, could not have been accidental, that a cause–effect relationship existed, and that the guilt must attach to the one who constructed this monstrous symbolic system, in which the two women had clashed with fatal results.

"I have committed a murder," Volodya repeated in despair, and he suddenly remembered Ivan Karamazov's conversation with the devil, and he remembered Smerdyakov, and then again Irina, who, however, was neither the devil nor Smerdyakov.[2] But did the devil exist? If he did, then he was nothing other than Volodya's predilec-

---

2. *Translator's note:* In Dostoyevsky's *The Brothers Karamazov*, Fyodor Mikhailovich Karamazov, the brothers' father, has a servant, Smerdyakov, who kills the father, his master, thinking that such was the wish of Ivan Karamazov, the oldest son. In addition, Ivan has a famous conversation with the devil in which he discusses the religious and philosophical questions that torment him.

tion for symbolism. But nothing existed, neither Smerdyakov, nor Ivan, nor the devil. Or rather, the devil exists because. . . . "And Irina! Anna Aleksandrovna. . . . Mama . . . it's all my fault! . . . the devil!"

This stream of thoughts was interrupted in the most surprising way. There rang out a sharp knock, or snapping sound. Volodya shuddered and turned his glazed eyes toward the place where the sound had arisen. He dimly understood and, grinning with a half-crazy smile, he said, quite like an madman, "Dead for a ducat, dead!" Only then did he finally realize that a mousetrap that he had placed under the sink the day before had snapped shut, a piece of lard serving as bait. The mouse was quite dead and lay in a small pool of blood. Volodya was surprised that he had just quoted Hamlet's words in the queen's bedchamber at the moment when the prince kills Polonius, pretending to go after a rat. He also recalled that the play that Hamlet puts on for Claudius carries the name *The Mousetrap*. This distracted Volodya and drew him out of his psychopathological state.

He went to his stepfather's apartment and took upon himself the entire burden of arranging the funeral. He called the necessary people, he ordered a wreath, and he arranged the wake. He cried. He embraced his father, his stepfather, and some other relatives. And he came to only after eight days, when he found himself sitting alone with his stepfather over a bottle of vodka.

"She was a saint," said his stepfather. "Yes, yes, a saint. I loved her," and he wiped away tears from his red cheeks.

"I was sometimes unfaithful to her—she knew about it . . . no, not that, that's not what I wanted to tell you. . . . She didn't love me. There. That's it, yes."

Volodya looked at his stepfather with astonishment, but he asked no questions.

"Well, yes, she had an affair, a fling, as they say. That was when we got married. It lasted only a few months. She said that it was like a brain disorder, an illness.

"Your mother," his stepfather said suddenly, completely soberly and distinctly, "loved only one person her entire life . . . (He paused, and Volodya froze, shutting his eyes) . . . your father."

Volodya's eyes opened wide. He sat shaken and stunned. It seemed to him that this was the most powerful experience of his life. For the rest of the evening, he neither spoke a word nor heard a word spoken by his stepfather. He did nothing but drink vodka, but he felt not the slightest effect. The stunned feeling did not go away.

At the institute, many people came up to Volodya to express their condolence. In answer he would murmur something inaudible. It was not clear if he heard the words spoken to him or even if he was aware of the person speaking. A few times Irina tenderly took his hand, but he evidently did not distinguish her from the others.

Later, when his attention was again directed to the outside world, Irina once more came up to him and said that if he needed her, she was at his disposal.

"Thank you," he answered indistinctly, not accepting her suggestion but, it seemed, not rejecting it, either. She waited a few days, but Volodya was silent. She thought it necessary to remind him that she was close by and that she wanted to help him. However, he again indistinctly thanked her and turned away.

The next time, Irina, almost publicly, in the corridor, placed her hand on his chest and said quietly and entreatingly:

"I need you, Volodya."

He looked up and saw that her black eyes had become still darker, filled with passion and sensuality.

He felt pity for her and said in a barely audible voice:

"I am not the same, Irina, not the man I was. Forgive me."

She walked away, biting her lip.

For a time Irina literally pursued Volodya. Haunting his every step, she gazed dog-like into his face but failed to perceive any changes in it. Well-intentioned people came up to Volodya and said,

"Keep it up!" "It serves her right!" "Now you see what she is." He lost his temper and said something coarse while thinking angrily, "Can there be no one who is able to pity her?"

Gradually, Volodya calmed down and the sky cleared, as it were. He lived now at a measured pace, without hurry. He took long walks, read Homer, and slept. At one point he had a dream which ended with his own words: "Well done, Professor Veisberg." Upon awakening, Volodya repeated consciously, but perplexedly, "Well done, Professor Veisberg." For the first time, he spoke the words without any irony. But remembering the occasion on which they had been said, he burst out laughing: In his dream he had seen his former mother-in-law, Natasha's mother.

His peace was now disturbed, and Volodya again became impulsive and impatient. He understood almost immediately what the dream meant for his life, and he did not hesitate long. A few days later he called Natasha, saying that he missed her and had to see her. Natasha agreed and invited him over.

Volodya arrived with a bouquet and presented it to Natasha (her mother was not home). They talked intimately and drank tea. Then Volodya stood up from the table and, in a voice trembling with emotion, said:

"Natasha, kiss me, remember, back then."

She was embarrassed and he hesitatingly embraced her. Natasha sought his lips, but he himself already pressed her to him. What was happening to her? Where did he learn that? How could it be? Impossible . . . impossible . . . impossible . . . dearest . . . beloved . . . you . . . you. . . .

"Again," Natasha whispered, shaken.

And they embraced again, and it was even better. Volodya undressed her. Even that was unusually new and fresh. He kissed her feet, her groin, her stomach, her shoulders, and, turning her over, her buttocks, her shoulder blades, and again her feet. Then, carefully squeezing her breast with his hand, he again found her lips, as their souls flew freely back and forth from one to the other through their open mouths. At the same time, their bodies pulsated in the dance that is pitiful and indecent in its imitations but that itself is beauty and sublimity incarnate. For the first time, they both felt that their merging was full and complete—both physically and spiritually.

Then they looked at each other happily. They did not leave off wanting to touch, to stroke, to kiss briefly, and to embrace passionately. He stroked her hair and shoulders, she moved her palm over his cheeks, he kissed her open palm, and she hugged his neck.

Natasha's mother arrived and instantly understood everything. They announced to her their intention to reunite. She burst into tears, but she was glad. Volodya stayed the night. In the morning, Natasha quickly gathered her things together and moved into Volodya's apartment.

Their days and nights were filled with rapture. Any separation seemed to them a parting. Once Volodya found Natasha crying, because he had come home fifteen minutes later than promised. Another time, Natasha sobbed bitterly: she had had a premonition that Volodya would be run over by a truck.

Then they got used to the idea that they were living in a harmonious marriage. They understood each other without completing their sentences and would smile quietly. The only thing that did not go well was Volodya's work. At first, the ecstasy of his honeymoon period got in the way, then Volodya became a bit lazy, and then he thought that he was basically not doing the work that was right for him. Suddenly he understood that he simply could not do anything, that he was not talented. No, people praised him as before or even more than before, but he himself knew the value of his work. He often had the same dream: a gloomy, winter landscape that begins to oppress his heart, and an empty, snow-covered field in the middle of which a dead scarecrow stands motionless. Rolling in the snow, Volodya approaches the scarecrow and sees that it is Natasha. She holds out to him a writhing hand so as to grab him, and he, still not awake, manages to realize that this is the end.

At one point, Volodya sat down at the table to work but, out of the blue, wrote the following lines with no corrections and without stopping to think:

> I will be neither young nor old—
> I am not alive: I vanished, I dimmed—
> Do I wait for news; will I endure this cold—
> All not for the first or for the last time.
>
> It will pierce again, and I'll be able to groan again,
> At table I will say a witty thing,
> I will still share laughter and sadness
> And I will disguise myself as the fool.
> Sadness will still demand a response
> In others' eyes—and I shall arrive.
> But I can know neither happiness nor unhappiness,
> I can be neither in heaven nor in hell.
>
> Not to live, but to feel; to have grown dim but not to perish,
> No, Lord, that's not for me to achieve!

He did not deceive himself for a moment about what he had written.

"Fourteen lines—a sonnet!" he thought disdainfully. It was not poetry—that was clear. It was a precise, clinical record. He understood this, and, folding the paper, he hid it away from his wife's eyes. He did not want her to read the history of his illness.

Recently, he had felt just that way, and, with his feelings put into verse, he began to think consciously about his condition: "I have not died, but I am not alive."

But soon after, his condition changed dramatically, and life became filled to the brim: Natasha was pregnant. Volodya had never before known such spiritual tension. The tenderness and gratitude that he felt for his wife were boundless. He often asked permission to place his ear to Natasha's stomach, and he would freeze as if standing over an abyss. Now Volodya discovered cosmic abysses everywhere. He thought about the mystery of conception and birth, about the role of each of the parents, and about the incomprehensible fact that he was giving life to a new human being, the fruit of such simple physical (well, perhaps chemical) interactions. Volodya again envied women. It seemed to him that at the moment of birth they were privy to all the mysteries of the universe. (Women that he had asked about this smiled as if speaking with a child who had posed a profound question beyond its years, and they confirmed his supposition, while confessing that all of that was immediately forgotten, wiped clean from memory.)

Natasha's pregnancy passed with unusual serenity and happiness. She was brought to the hospital in plenty of time, and the next day she gave birth to a girl. Volodya fell into utter bliss. He was unable to do anything on his own, so that his stepfather never left him alone. Together they made the necessary purchases, and together, on the eve of Natasha's discharge from the hospital, they got properly soused.

That morning, Volodya went to the market to buy flowers for his wife, anticipating that soon, within a half hour, he would take his daughter in his arms. After buying flowers, Volodya tried to hail a taxi, but there were none about. He suddenly became nervous, and, seeing a green light on the other side of the street, he ran toward it. In that second, he was hit by a truck hurtling around the corner. . . .

Oh, my God. . . . He died on the spot in two minutes. . . . I can't believe what I'm saying. . . . He never regained consciousness. . . . Natasha waited for him the whole day. . . . What have I been talking about? . . . God help us. . . . What in hell is going on here? . . . Oh, yes, now I remember. . . . Freud has been rehabilitated. . . . Oh, you devil. . . . You damned, damned devil!

1980–1981

BAKHTIN AND OTHERS

*B*akhtin was planning to spend the summer in the country. He wanted to rent a room with a small porch, and it had to be somewhere not far from Moscow so that he would be able, without strain, to transport the books he needed for his work. Bakhtin had an idea for an article on the theory of literary prototypes. Even though success had eluded him thus far, he believed that he was on the verge of teasing out the laws governing the transition a character makes from life to literature, and that these laws must be nearly as fixed as those governing transposition in music. In the country, the article would go well. There he was always able to do good work—even the mosquitoes helped. You slap yourself on the forehead when an idea occurs to you. And where else do you slap yourself on the forehead as often as in the country, fighting off mosquitoes?

Bakhtin already had a telephone number, procured by friends, which he was supposed to call. He was to ask for Nikolai Fyodorovich, so as to come to an agreement on just the sort of room he needed. Nikolai Fyodorovich invited him to come and inspect the accommodations and the yard. From the train station, he was instructed to walk along Professors Cul-De-Sac, and then along Leskov (formerly Kaganovich) Street (this was important since there was also a Leskov Lane, and if you did not say "formerly Kaganovich," you might be sent to the wrong place), then, at the corner of Prishvin Street and Architect Rudnev Street, to boldly push open the gate with the number 17.

While he waited for Bakhtin, Nikolai Fyodorovich was digging up the garden beds, and Bakhtin at once enthusiastically offered to help him with it.

"You called yourself by your last name, but, excuse me, what are your first name and patronymic?" asked the owner. He was of middle height and middle age, fair-haired with a hint of red, with small green eyes and a penetrating glance. Freckles were just barely noticeable on his face and hands. Lively, blond eyebrows came together above a delicate, slightly hooked nose. His thin lips were striking not so much for their narrowness as for their length. When they parted, an incredible, black abyss of a mouth opened up, which would have seemed altogether frightful without the noble form of the finely molded chin.

"My name is Maxim Menandrovich," said Bakhtin.

"Maxim . . . excuse me?"

"Menandrovich."

"Menandrovich? What sort of name is that?"

"There was such a name in Old Russia. From the ancient Greek."

"What does it mean?"

"In Greek, Menander means 'masculine strength.'"

"Aha!" Nikolai Fyodorovich said, with a spontaneous chuckle. "But permit me to ask, what do they call your father at home?"

"My father is dead," Bakhtin said. "But at home people called him Andryusha. If it is hard for you to remember my patronymic, you may use Andreyich, but even better, just call me Maxim."

"For goodness sake, Maxim Menandrovich, how can you suggest such a thing? It is a genuine pleasure to pronounce your complete name and patronymic: Maxim Menandrovich Bakhtin," Nikolai

Fyodorovich said, articulating his words slowly and solemnly and making a gesture with his hand as if introducing a guest to a large gathering.

"And pardon me, but what might be your profession?" the owner continued to inquire.

"I'm a philologist," Maxim answered.

"That means . . . I didn't catch it, you study birds, or the weather, or maybe literature?"

"I'm not an ornithologist or a phenologist, but a philologist—which means literature."

"Really, my goodness, how interesting! I envy you, I do," Nikolai Fyodorovich said, grinning. "Me, I'm just an engineer, a simple engineer."

"And I'm just a simple literary scholar," Bakhtin said in self-defense.

"Ah, no, no, don't say that, literature is . . . you know, literature . . . not everyone has what it takes. I respect you, I really do. Lyovushka!" the simple engineer who respected literature suddenly called out. "Lyovushka! Come here."

A tall boy of about 13 came out of the house. He was red-haired, heavily freckled, with a large mouth and protruding ears.

"May I present my son, Lev," said Nikolai Fyodorovich, and glanced searchingly at Bakhtin.

"Lev Nikolayevich," Maxim said, smiling, having passed the examination.[1]

"Yes, absolutely right," the proud father confirmed. "Not Tolstoy, of course. We are Pavlovs, but still and all. . . . Lyovushka, please show Maxim . . . um . . . Menandrovich his room."

---

1. *Translator's note*: The examination consists in finding out whether Maxim will recognize that the boy has the same first name and patronymic as Leo (Lev Nikolayevich) Tolstoy.

"What do you say. Let's go, Lev Nikolayevich," Bakhtin said, putting his arm around the boy's shoulders.

"Let's go," the boy said, in a voice that was somehow weak. Freeing himself from Maxim's arm, he walked down the path toward the house.

The room turned out to be cozy, although a bit damp. In it were a fairly wide trestle bed, a small bedside table, a round table covered with an oil cloth, an easy chair, two straight chairs, and a wardrobe.

"So, this room," Lyova said, as if he were reluctantly repeating lessons he had long ago learned by rote. "It's still damp, as you can see, but the fact is, the house has not yet fully warmed up. We haven't had many sunny days yet, and we've only fired up the stove once. We'll fire it up a few more times—the stove is behind this wall, in Grandfather's room—and everything will be okay. All the dampness will disappear. And here is the porch. You can put a folding bed here, or anything you want, and here's the refrigerator. East is to the left, so, you see, the sun is on the porch from sunup to sundown."

"Good, very good," said Maxim. "But by the way, where do you yourself spend the summer? Do you go somewhere or stay here in your summer house?"

"Actually, I wanted to go to Pioneer camp, but they said I had to stay here, that they had no one to leave Grandfather with, that he is sick and over 80. I said, but why are you taking on a lodger? He can keep an eye on Grandfather. But they said that I was being ridiculous, that there was no alternative, and that Grandfather loves me so much. 'You'll be together,' they said. So it seems I have to spend the summer here."

"But what about your parents? Won't they be coming to the summer house?"

"No, they come only on Saturdays and Sundays. Mama says that after work she can't run to the far corners of the earth."

"So what do you say, Lev Nikolayevich. We'll look after your grandfather together. And by the way, what is his name?"

Lyova paused, and then, quickly looking at Bakhtin, he said:

"His name is Fyodor Mikhailovich."[2]

"What?" Bakhtin choked.

"Fyodor Mikhailovich."

"Ah," Bakhtin said, drawing out his words and then suddenly bursting out laughing. "Listen, now I know the names of your son and grandson! Shall I tell you?"

"Why not," the boy said almost lazily, and he waited expectantly.

"Your son's name will be Seryozha, so he will be Sergei L'vovich, and of course, Sergei L'vovich will become the father of Sasha—Aleksandr Sergeyevich! Right?"[3]

"How did you know?" Lyova said embarrassedly.

"But isn't that the way it is?"

"Papa told me that that is the way it has to be, that it was planned long ago."

"And how do you yourself feel about this?"

"I really don't know. I never thought about it. I just don't like everybody calling me Lev Nikolayevich."

"You don't like your name?"

"It's a name like any other. But my neighbor over here is called Mitka, and Irka lives over there, and Styopka a bit further, but I am—Lev Nikolayevich."

"So? It's a worthy name."

"Worthy?" the future grandfather of Aleksandr Sergeyevich burst out angrily. "And would you like it if your full name also became

---

2. *Translator's note*: This is the name and patronymic of Dostoyevsky.

3. *Translator's note*: Sergei L'vovich Pushkin was the father of Russia's national poet, Alexander Sergeyevich Pushkin—whose nickname was Sasha.

your nickname? Because Lev Nikolayevich *is* my nickname! They should call me Lyova!" He was almost crying.

Bakhtin was surprised at the depth not only of the boy's suffering but also of his philological insight into names and nicknames. The situation where name and nickname coincide suddenly appeared to him quite as awful as the situation of Oedipus after he discovers that his own children are also his siblings.

"Lev Nikolayevich!" A voice sounded beyond the wall that separated Maxim's room from the owner's chambers. "Bring our guest to me."

"Grandfather lives there," said the boy in a whisper, and then replied loudly. "Right this minute, Fyodor Mikhailovich!" And with a gesture of invitation, using the same tone to Bakhtin, he said, "If you please."

They went through the porch into the yard, circled round the house, and ended up at the entrance to the owner's half. On the way, Bakhtin thought uneasily that Fyodor Mikhailovich had heard his entire conversation with the grandson, including, in all likelihood, the boy's complaints, and yet he had called out to Lev in such a way as to cause him displeasure. Lyova immediately began to play the fool. He was obviously preparing an obsequious and saccharine performance of some kind.

"Is the playacting for him or for me?" Maxim asked himself.

"Here we are, sir," said the boy. "Allow me to make the introductions: Fyodor Mikhailovich—Maxim Menandrovich."

He started to giggle.

"It really is funny," Bakhtin said, understanding the boy and smiling.

"Pleased to meet you, very pleased to meet you," said the old man, rising from his chair and scraping along in his slippers as he moved toward Maxim.

Quite small in stature, bent over, but somehow fresh and clean, smooth shaven, with rosy cheeks, Fyodor Mikhailovich squeezed and shook his guest's hand a long time, saying over and over, "Delighted to make your acquaintance!"

Maxim scrutinized the old man. Gray hair parted in the straightest of lines, white (not gray) protruding eyebrows, intelligent green eyes, a nose with a hint of eagleness, long thin lips, a well-shaped, narrow chin, hands in motion with rust-colored age spots, a most noble countenance, a voice with a pleasant timbre and without a trace of hoarseness (he had never smoked).

"Please have a seat," Fyodor Mikhailovich said. "I heard that you are studying Dostoyevsky?"

To answer in the affirmative to this question, posed by Fyodor Mikhailovich, the grandfather of Lev Nikolayevich and great-grandfather of Aleksandr Sergeyevich, was absolutely impossible, so Maxim said evasively:

"I study 19th-century Russian literature."

"And therefore also Dostoyevsky?"

"I am more interested in questions of theory."

"Excuse me, but I remember reading Bakhtin's studies of Dostoyevsky's poetics. Is he a relative of yours?"

"No," Maxim responded monosyllabically.

He was always embarrassed when people mentioned Bakhtin to him, but today it had become phantasmagorical. What a bacchanalia of names! Maxim understood that without intending to he had entered into the system in regular operation in the Pavlov family, that he filled out a missing element in that system. He even joined the clan, forming a secondary, but important branch of the genealogical tree. Fyodor Mikhailovich, with a reproachful glance at Bakhtin, made it clear to him that it was no use to resist.

"I assume you brought a deposit with you," the old man said, changing the subject. "All financial affairs go through me."

"Yes, of course. Here you are."

"And when do you propose to pay the remaining sum?"

"I had supposed at the end of my stay, but perhaps you would like to proceed somewhat differently."

"Yes, it would be best for me to receive it from you immediately upon moving in. And then for gas and electricity at the end of the summer."

This conflicted with several of Bakhtin's plans. Moreover, he was hearing for the first time about supplemental charges for gas and electricity. Nevertheless, he maintained his silence and nodded his head in affirmation.

As this conversation was taking place, Lyovushka sat at the table. First he carefully drew lines on a small sheet of paper and then filled it with a drawing. Bakhtin tried to make out the drawing but he could not discern anything.

"What are you doing there, Lev Nikolayevich?" the grandfather asked.

"I'm just . . . nothing, Fyodor Mikhailovich," the boy answered and hid the paper.

"He's always drawing something or other," the old man explained. "And the results are not bad. . . . So, we have settled everything. When are you going to move in?"

"In a week, I think," said Bakhtin, and he bowed. Lyova went to see him out.

"Can I take a look at your drawing?" Maxim asked.

"It's nothing, it's not a drawing at all."

"What is it then?"

"My friends and I have a game. We draw bank notes."

"Counterfeit notes, you mean?"

"Sort of."

"Show me?"

"Okay."

Maxim took the piece of paper held out to him. On it was written in English, "One Dollar," and it looked very much like the real thing, only instead of George Washington there was Dostoyevsky, drawn to a likeness, but in such a way that from his visage stared Fyodor Mikhailovich, the grandfather of Lev Nikolayevich. But that was not the only thing that stunned Bakhtin. Looking at the bank note produced by the young artist, he understood that the portrait of Fyodor Mikhailovich was also to a certain extent a self-portrait.

"Would you be willing to make me a present of this money?" Bakhtin inquired.

"What's it to you?" Lyova asked absently. But then he suddenly came to life and added, "But as you wish. Only not to give but to sell."

"Sell? How strange! How much do you want?"

"Twenty kopeks—exactly the amount I need for something."

"Why not? It's a deal."

Lyova looked all around to see if there were witnesses and then took the coin, showing by his demeanor that one should be quiet about a completed transaction. Bakhtin smiled knowingly and made it clear that he considered that he had the better of the bargain, as indeed he did, although from the point of view of pedagogy, the exchange of currency could only be seen as a dubious undertaking, and both participants in the transaction knew this.

Nikolai Fyodorovich came out of the barn and asked, "And so, Maxim Menandrovich, you're leaving already?"

"Yes, I have to go."

"But I thought we could have some tea together. My wife, Lyudmila Grigoriyevna, is coming soon and will organize tea with jam for us."

"Thanks, but I can't. I've absolutely got to be in Moscow in an hour."

"A great pity. We could sit for a bit and talk. You could tell us interesting things about literature, about writers. We are all passionate lovers of art."

"I'm a mediocre storyteller, and besides, I am attracted to quite dry, academic questions, so it's unlikely my conversation would prove entertaining for you."

"I notice that you are always overmodest. Or maybe, humility is greater than pride? Anyway, a pity. So, good-bye then. Till next Saturday."

"Good-bye!" said Maxim, noting in passing that Nikolai Fyodorovich somehow had known what had been said in Fyodor Mikhailovich's room about moving in, just as the old man evidently had known what Bakhtin had discussed with his son while the latter was digging in the flower bed.

"That means they also already know about my exchange with Lyova," Maxim thought to himself, and a wondrous sensation of mystery touched his soul. Bakhtin loved this sensation almost more than anything else in life, although for him it was always surrounded by a sadness that was at the same time both exhausting and light. But this fleeting presentiment of a mystery lay under the heavy weight of an undefined something: a tension built up in his heart and communicated itself to his entire body nearly to the point of causing an involuntary muscular contraction. Maxim tried to chase away this unexpected and inexplicable uneasiness, and he spent the entire way back on the train thinking about his forthcoming article. Bakhtin did not even notice immediately that everyone had left the train, he was so taken up by his new thought, which seemed to him both fruitful and capable of setting his now-stagnating work in motion.

A person does not possess completeness, Bakhtin thought. Only a character has that, meaning a character who has passed through the crucible of the plot. Only the plot, as a kind of unity, imparts to the character wholeness and completeness. Therefore, in order to obtain completeness, a person needs an author, that is, a certain other. The writer-author, writing about his person-self, splits himself in two, describing himself as someone else, alienating himself from himself. Otherwise it would be impossible to become a character— even in one's own writing. However, in order to become a character, this other, this not-I, has somehow to enter the author and become a part of him, his double, his embryo. The other enters the author as spirit, as the breath of life, and becomes flesh within him— condensing and solidifying. Then the author squeezes this clot out of himself, cutting its facets with reversals of fortune, giving it form with intrigues, baking it with *mises en scènes*, making clear its essence through relationships with things and with other characters. Finally, he separates himself from it, locking it up in the story as in a cage.

Maxim was glad. His new thought pleased him, and it seemed to him that he would be able to formulate it with precision and elegance. He was also amused that in a way he was indebted to his meeting with the Pavlov family for this new train of thought. However, as he was walking home from the train, Maxim suddenly began to feel anxious: What if he was not acting independently? He even began to feel uncomfortable at the thought of where he should look for the sources of his idea, and he decided not to examine the coincidences. Nevertheless, he had hardly entered his apartment when he took down from the shelf a volume of M. M. Bakhtin and read: "In all aesthetic forms, the organizing force is the value category of the Other, i.e., the relation to the Other, enriched by the surplus value of vision for transgrediential completion. The author becomes close to the hero only in the absence of the purity of valuational self-consciousness, where such self-consciousness is dominated by the consciousness of the Other." Maxim felt ashamed and humiliated, and "the transgrediential completion" was a hard slap in the face. Furthermore, it was clear that the slap proceeded from none other than Fyodor Mikhailovich; he immediately remembered the reproachful glance of the old man when Maxim responded negatively to the question about being Bakhtin's relation. Attempting to salvage his honor, Maxim began to argue to himself that the author-hero relation was taken by him in reverse perspective, from the point of view not of the author but of the hero. It was the character who looks for the Other and finds the author, into whom he enters, bringing him to the point of insanity, of possession, actually requiring exorcisms to drive out the uninvited, solidified foreign spirit, which abandons the author and becomes his often horrible, terrifying, and threatening double. The author is passive. It is the character that acts and rages. Regarding susceptibility to raving, Bakhtin set creation nearly on a par with possession by spirits, although he had earlier always supposed that art made any search for proofs of the existence of God irrelevant. What other arguments were necessary? There he is—God. Now, however, Maxim himself resembled one possessed, and in that state he was distinctly conscious that, if they tried to drive out the demon that possessed him, the little devil inside him would answer to one name only. He felt chills as he said the name to himself: Fyodor Mikhailovich. Pronouncing it, Maxim indeed calmed himself, as if a demon, bearing that name and carrying out the rules of the ceremony, had passed from him.

"Not a bad exorcism." Bakhtin laughed. "Get out, Fyodor Mikhailovich!" And he felt himself drawn to the summer house.

The whole week he made his preparations as if in a hurry. In the middle of getting his things together, he would suddenly be seized by a thought and would sit at his desk. He would get up from his writing in the middle of a word just to put some trifle into his bag; after that he would cross out what he had just written, and then he would jump up again. He was by now not sure that he would be able to work well at the summer place, but he knew that it was *necessary* to move there. On Saturday, he went. They were waiting for him. At the gate stood Lyova, in the yard Nikolai Fyodorovich greeted him, through the veranda window Fyodor Mikhailovich waved his hand, and out of the summer kitchen came Lyudmila Grigoriyevna smiling and taking off her apron as she went.

"Welcome!" said Nikolai Fyodorovich. "So, let me introduce you: our mistress of the house!"

"Hello, Lyudmila Grigoriyevna!"

"Pleased to meet you, Maxim Menandrovich!" the mistress said, throwing up her eyelashes.

One was immediately aware of a mixture of energy and embarrassment in this woman. There was something nearly impudent in her features, to go along with an unmistakable shyness in the expression on her face. Uncontrollable black hair on her shoulders; black, seemingly frightened, eyes; a nervous mouth; veins that stood out on her neck (one vein throbbed, Maxim noted); coarse hands; heavy feet. Bakhtin did not spend any more time on this scrutinizing than was polite, but on turning back to the house, he managed to catch the persistent and interested gaze of Fyodor Mikhailovich, who abruptly turned his eyes away.

"It is beginning," Bakhtin thought, for some reason.

"You go unpack, Maxim Menandrovich, and I'll set the table," said Lyudmila Grigoriyevna.

"Please, don't go to any trouble. I wouldn't want to be a burden to you."

"There's nothing at all burdensome about it. We have dinner at this hour," Nikolai Fyodorovich intervened. "And I hope that you will do us the honor."

"Thank you."

"Maybe I can help you unpack your books?" Lyova asked.

"Sure, let's go."

Maxim began laying out his things. Lyova did not even think of taking part in this.

"Here are my books. Take a look if you want."

"I've already seen them. Nothing interesting."

"Then why did you ask?"

"I . . . no, nothing." The boy waited until his interlocutor looked at him, and then shot a warning glance in the direction of the wall, behind which was his grandfather's room.

Bakhtin understood that he was to keep silent, but Lyova began to speak in a rapid whisper.

"Grandfather secretly observed that you gave me 20 kopecks and complained to Father. Father was unsure how to deal with me. I heard how he consulted with Mother. He said maybe it's all right and appropriate, but she for some reason kept repeating, 'Make him give it back, make him give it back.' So Father ordered me to give it back."

He stopped. The pause lasted a while.

"So, what . . . ?" Lyova asked softly.

"What do you mean?"

"Give it back?"

Maxim shrugged his shoulders.

"Then here's what we'll do. I will now say loudly that it's agreed and then I'll pretend to return your money. Over there, they're all waiting. They're looking in at the window."

Maxim stole a glance and saw that Lev Nikolayevich was right. Meanwhile, the latter coughed and said:

"Last time, I borrowed 20 kopecks from you, so now I'm returning it," and he rapped the coin on the table, but in the same instant he raked it into his palm and said voicelessly, "So, I can keep it, okay?"

Bakhtin nodded, finding himself already a second time caught in a pedagogical embarrassment.

"Give some sort of answer," the boy whispered.

"Hm, if you don't need it anymore. Have you already made some sort of arrangement?"

"Yes, thank you, I wanted to buy a stamp."

"And so, did you buy it?"

"No."

"Why not?"

"You see, Styopka had already sold it."

"Besides stamps, do you collect anything else?

"Also old money."

"Aha, I thought so. Then I have a present for you. Take that book over there, you see? There should be a bookmark in it. Find it? It's an assignation from the 1860s. Nastasya Filippovna burned that sort of money up."

"Burned up? How's that, in an oven?"

"You don't understand," Bakhtin said, laughing. "For some reason I decided that you had already read *The Idiot*. Nastasya Filippovna is the heroine of that novel."

"I have read only *The Double*. I didn't like it."

"But why precisely *The Double*?"

"Grandfather gave it to me to read. . . . Thanks for the assignation."

"Perhaps it will compensate you for the loss of the stamp."

"Yes, thank you."

"Lyovushka!" Lyudmila Grigoriyevna called out. "Invite Maxim Menandrovich to the table!"

At the table the conversation continued to revolve around literature, no matter how much Bakhtin tried to turn it in another direction. Lyudmila Grigoriyevna told about a coworker who was selected for the union steering committee and who, instead of raffling off a volume of Dostoyevsky's correspondence with his wife, had brazenly walked off with it. But not to worry. Nikolai Fyodorovich located a copy, although he had to pay a bit too much for it. Nikolai Fyodorovich remarked that Anna Grigoriyevna[4] had given the letters to the publisher in mutilated form. She marked them up, so that to this day there's no making them out. There's women for you. But Fyodor

---

4. *Translator's note*: The wife of Fyodor Mikhailovich Dostoyevsky.

Mikhailovich expressed an interest in the correspondence between Dostoyevsky and Suslov, had it been found? Bakhtin reluctantly answered that he had heard that there was living in Leningrad an old book dealer who held that correspondence in his hands and with the same hands had destroyed it, fearing the publication of intimate materials.

Bakhtin's knowledgeableness brought inconcealable delight to Lyudmila Grigoriyevna, but the information being communicated provoked the wrath of all present. Bakhtin was on the point of utter boredom, but Lyovushka stepped in and told a story he had recently heard in school about a rabbit. Maxim looked at him with gratitude, as the parents glanced at their son reproachfully.

They thanked Bakhtin for the conversation. He, for his part, thanked them for dinner and then set out on his first walk. However, as he was returning about two hours later, right in front of him a group of people rushed shouting into the room in a tangled mass: two boys, one of whom was Lev Nikolayevich, a man and a woman. Entering behind them, Maxim heard:

"I was not stealing! It wasn't me!" (Lyovushka was shouting.)

"Then who? Who took it?"

"How should I know? It wasn't me who took your bike. I have my own, and I don't give a fig for yours!"

"You took it, you did! You're the only one! No one else was there."

"Styopka was there!"

"Styopka didn't take it!"

"And I didn't take it!"

The woman shouted shrilly:

"Parents, do something! Your son stole a bicycle and hid it somewhere."

"Do you want us to punish him?" Lyudmila Grigoriyevna asked.

"That's your business. We need the bicycle."

"Does that mean you want to search the house?" said Nikolai

Fyodorovich, entering the conversation. "Or will you permit us to get to the bottom of it ourselves?"

"Nikolai Fyodorovich," the man said, in conciliation. "Here in the village it is no secret from anyone that your son has attacks of kleptomania. So, you understand, we came to you."

"Are you saying, then, that you do not suspect me of anything?"

"For pity's sake, Nikolai Fyodorovich!"

"Then with your permission, we will clear everything up ourselves and if we find the bicycle, Lyova will return it to you immediately. Good day!"

"Good-bye."

They left. Bakhtin was not about to wait for the interrogation and perhaps the punishment, which was bound to follow, so he went to his half of the house. He sat on the veranda and tried to concentrate, but that was difficult. Excited voices reached him, and he saw how they opened first the barn, then the kitchen and various outbuildings, searching for the bicycle. Maxim went into his room in order not to look out the window, and he froze on the threshold: next to the trestle bed stood a bicycle. Maxim had the impulse to carry it out that instant into the courtyard, but he thought twice.

"Why did Lyova put the bicycle here?" he asked himself. "Was it because I was not home and the boy figured that he would manage to get it out before I arrived? Or does he see in me if not an accomplice, then an indulgent well-wisher? But of course, he knows that I have already uncovered his prank. Does that mean that I in fact am his accomplice in a certain sense? Amusing! But maybe I really should inform on him. Let's wait a bit."

The search outside the window continued. Lyova wept and swore on oath, but no one believed him. Fyodor Mikhailovich from time to time cried out from his room:

"It was he. I swear it was he! For shame!"

71

When the grandfather next shouted something similar out the window, Lyova suddenly said, with nearly unrestrained ferocity:

"If you, Fyodor Mikhailovich, were a kleptomaniac in your youth, that does not at all mean that I am obliged to repeat your life experience with all of your errors and flaws! I am not Fyodor Mikhailovich! I am Lev Nikolayevich!"

Everyone was struck dumb except Nikolai Fyodorovich, who gave his son a box on the ears. The grandfather was simply speechless and throttled his emotion.

What stunned Bakhtin was that, in his opinion as a philologist, the ferocious speech of Lev Nikolayevich had been prepared beforehand and rehearsed many times in private. He went out onto the porch. The boy threw him a wan look.

"I think," Maxim said, "it's pointless to look for the bicycle. One of the boys must have borrowed it for a time, and now, quite possibly, it is standing against the fence of its owner's house. Would you like me to go and have a look later?"

"Why should this trouble you?" Lyudmila Grigoriyevna protested.

But he convinced everyone of the expediency of this step, and, having waited a minute, when no one was looking, he walked the bicycle out and onto "Former Kaganovich," where he informed its owners that he had found it by the fence. When he returned, Lyovushka, having waited by the gate, seized his hand and rapidly raised it to his lips.

"Thank you," he whispered. "That's forever."

His first day in the country had exhausted Bakhtin, and he began to prepare for the night. It was necessary to exercise care in moving about the room; behind the partition slept Fyodor Mikhailovich. Bakhtin heard it when the old man turned over and when he grunted. When Maxim lay down, his head to the wall, the sounds from the neighboring room became more distinct. The grandfather groaned for a bit, muttered something, and then suddenly in a tragic whisper cried out, "Lord, why? Why, Lord?"

After a pause he again began to mutter, "The pain, God, such pain! I can't go on."

Maxim started to think that Fyodor Mikhailovich was complaining about his illness, but from the succeeding lamentations it became clear that he was enduring suffering of quite a different sort.

"Not a bit of love, not the slightest affection," the old man lamented. "Or even so much as obedience?"

His voice began to ring out.

"I say: Obedience, where is it? Respect for father, for grandfather? Lev Nikolayevich, my grandson! Or that . . . what, doesn't she remember? Has she forgotten everything? At least a crumb of gratitude! And the result! If a son, one's own son. . . ."

It did not seem likely that the groaning behind the wall would end any time soon, so Bakhtin covered his head with the blanket. In making the lamentations indistinct, this action also turned them into something like a rumbling. Sleep came, which was interrupted by the robust, shrill, beautiful voice of Fyodor Mikhailovich:

"Eight o'clock! Get up! Lev Nikolayevich, reveille!"

"Father, don't make noise," said Nikolai Fyodorovich. "You have no idea about Maxim Menandrovich's habits. Maybe he wants to sleep late in the morning."

"Summer! A sunny day!" the old man exclaimed. "What kind of person sleeps at such an hour? Maxim Menandrovich has proper habits—I know."

Bakhtin generally worked at night and loved to sleep late in the morning hours. He supposed that it would also be like that in the country, but for some reason he felt awkward about it. Having more than once thought that his way of life was incorrect, he decided that here was the opportunity to alter his habits. When he went out to the sink, with soap dish and toothbrush, Fyodor Mikhailovich greeted him with a brilliant smile:

"Good morning! How did you sleep in a new place?"

"Well, thank you. And how was your night?"

"Excellent, excellent! You know, I am now in great form."

Bakhtin shifted from one leg to the other, waiting to be allowed to wash. He could not stand it if someone watched while he brushed his teeth. However, it seemed that Fyodor Mikhailovich was feeling compelled to explain how Maxim should perform precisely this activity.

"Wash up, wash up! I'm certainly not disturbing you, am I?"

Bakhtin shook his head and began to wash up. The old man waited for the moment when Maxim had stuffed his mouth with toothpaste to ask:

"And what about the mosquitoes? Didn't bother you?"

"Mmm. . . ."

"Right, there are not many of them yet. They come out a bit later. Did you bring some sort of repellent with you?"

"Mmm. . . ."

"You know, that's quite a necessary thing. . . . But, wash up, wash up, I'll go have tea. If you want, I'll put on your kettle, but then don't forget to turn off the stove so as not to waste gas."

Maxim finished washing up, carried his towel into his room, and considered which shirt to put on. But at that moment Fyodor Mikhailovich rapped at the window. In his hands was a kettle.

"It's boiling, it's boiling," he said angrily. "Here, you know, we have very heat-efficient gas. So you've got to see to it that it doesn't burn for nothing."

Maxim soon learned the ropes of country living, he adapted himself to it, and although he often forgot about the supernatural heat efficiency of the gas in the kitchen, he did not violate the locally observed customs for the duration. Whatever he needed to use, he put back in its place. He brought the old man medicine from Moscow.

He inquired of Lev Nikolayevich as to his life in school. And on Saturdays he met Lyudmila Grigoriyevna and Nikolai Fyodorovich. Finally, he began to write his article, since it was for its sake, he supposed, that he had come to the country.

*   *   *

One evening Bakhtin was working late when suddenly, in the evening quiet, a voice clearly sounded that revealed tension and violent emotion.

"No, Maxim, no, no!"

Bakhtin went out and stood rooted to the ground. There, drenched in moonlight, stood Lyovushka. He was in his underwear, having come right from his bed. His face was contorted from crying, like an infant's, and his body shook with violent trembling, but not from cold. His eyes were open, but if they saw anything, it was not distinctly.

"Don't feel sorry for me, Maxim," he cried out. "I'm trash! I'm a kleptomaniac!"

Maxim quietly went up to him, carefully took the boy by the shoulders, and said softly:

"Back to bed, Lyovushka."

But Lyovushka shook off Bakhtin's hand and shouted:

"And you, Grandfather, don't touch me, understand? Do you get it, Fyodor Mikhailovich? You repulsive double! Am I anything at all, sir? You're right, I'm nothing. That's just the way it is. You only get stupid things from me, sir."

Maxim again put his arms around Lev and touched his lips to the boy's forehead—no fever. "Somnambulism," Bakhtin realized.

"Let's go, my friend, let's go."

"A—a, Styopka! So go ahead, try it! Call me Lev Nikolayevich once more, just try it!"

The boy had to be awakened. As it was, he was not going back; he was resisting, pushing Bakhtin away with unchildlike force, smiling, crying, threatening, repenting, several times mentioning Maxim, speaking to him using "ty" without the patronymic. Finally, he saw Bakhtin distinctly:

"Maxim Menandrovich?" he asked, surprised. "What are you doing out here?"

"Well, I got caught up in working and I came out to stretch my legs. And you?"

"I . . . to take a piss."

"So go ahead, piss away, don't be shy."

"Good night, Maxim Menandrovich!"

"Sleep well, Lyovushka!"

Bakhtin watched the boy walk away. Within him arose a paternal feeling, which warmed him with its tenderness but at the same time scalded him with alarm.

"How does he live?" Bakhtin thought. "What are the injuries that torment him, what are the sorrows?"

In the morning, he asked:

"How are you feeling?"

"Fine," Lyovushka answered, surprised.

"And how did you sleep?"

"Okay."

"Did you have any dreams?"

"No, I didn't. I rarely have any dreams. Wish I did."

"Did you see what a moon we had last night?"

"No, I slept without waking up. Why do you ask?"

"It seemed to me that you went out during the night while I was working—to take a leak, probably."

"No, I was sleeping. And you?"

"What about me?"

"Did you have any dreams?"

"No, I don't think so, no. But wait. I did, of course, I did have a dream. A strange one. A childhood dream. I was flying. They say that when children dream they are flying, it means they are growing. I haven't been growing for a long time, but there I was, flying. I dreamed I saw a river flowing near a mountain—not the river near here—and I had to fly from a precipice to the other bank. I threw out my arms and flew, but I didn't quite make it to the other bank and fell with my legs in the water, and the water was cold. I think my blanket slid down and my legs froze."

"A nice dream. In my dreams, if I fly, I always fall. I plummet from a high place. But that way, to throw out my arms . . . no, it's never happened."

Bakhtin's heart trembled.

"You know what," he said. "I have a tent. Let's stock up on potatoes and jam, and go on a hike. We'll be back by evening. There, somewhere between the river and the forest, we'll make a fire, cook the potatoes, lie about in the tent, and then head for home, how about it?"

"Really? When?"

"Right now. How long can it take to pack? Fifteen minutes to get your things together."

"Right away. I'll just go tell Grandfather. Right now."

He ran away and returned in ten minutes.

"I can't go," he said, turning his eyes away.

"Why not?"

"Grandfather isn't letting me. He says that he can't stay alone the entire day."

"What a shame," Bakhtin said, lingering on the sound. "How did I not foresee that?"

He was unable to come up with a replacement for the hike, so he turned away in embarrassment, as if he had been responsible for the failure of his idea.

As later became clear, the boy's parents, like his grandfather, had for some reason also not approved of Maxim's idea. And he never again invited Lev even on short walks. He went out by himself.

* * *

Maxim took walks in a forest that residents of the village considered to be far away and to which they went only when the mushroom-picking season began. It was deserted there even on Saturdays and Sundays, and the sensation of blissful seclusion expanded the chest like a deep breath. While wandering in the forest, Maxim invented a game and played it with himself. He would choose a tree in a clearing and would walk toward it, imagining that someone was standing behind it. That someone was supposed to come out from behind without waiting for Maxim to get to the tree. The game consisted in correctly predicting the moment the stranger would come out from the concealed position, as well as in describing as clearly as possible his or her external appearance, character traits, and, of course, gender. It sometimes happened that Bakhtin would draw the most detailed portrait of the person behind the tree, but at the moment when the portrait subject should have appeared in the open, Bakhtin's imagination would unexpectedly and playfully pull a switch on him, substituting something completely different. It occasionally happened that Maxim simply could not guess in which second his partner would emerge from behind the tree. But after a series of exercises, Maxim noticed that the players came out at the same moment that his own heart gave him a sign, a peculiar sort of fluttering sensation. He did not lose any more. But then his imagination on its own made the game more complex, and people started appearing from behind different trees—not from behind those that had been designated at the beginning. It was impossible to understand which result was better, victory or defeat. It was also impossible to stop playing, although Bakhtin many times thought that this tree would be the last one. He was even getting tired of all this, but when he approached the last "last tree" at the very edge of the forest, he heard voices and thought that this was the result of exhaustion. Until now, the players had not spoken.

But he quickly came to and immediately realized that the voices were real, a man's and a woman's. The man was being accusatory, and the woman was apologizing plaintively. Maxim wanted to avoid the quarreling pair, but he found it impossible to reach the road without an encounter. Coming closer, he heard the man use obscene language, while the woman—whom Bakhtin, after glimpsing her face, recognized as Lyudmila Grigoriyevna—imploringly pressed her hands together and swallowed her tears. At the same moment, the man—and Bakhtin also recognized him as the owner of one of the summer houses in the village—slapped Lyudmila Grigoriyevna in the face, in a short but powerful motion. She cried out, and Maxim rushed toward her, but she, noticing him before her companion did, managed to make a warning gesture and, instantaneously adopting a mask of tranquility, said in modulated tones:

"How nice, Maxim Menandrovich, that we have met. Let's go home together."

The man turned to Bakhtin. His face still showed the traces of his anger. He silently nodded and plunged into the forest. Lyudmila Grigoriyevna took Maxim's arm and they went along the road to the village.

"Why didn't you let me teach that scoundrel a lesson?" Bakhtin asked.

"He isn't a scoundrel," she replied. "It's me . . . I very much . . . I insulted him terribly."

"Be that as it may," Bakhtin grumbled. "To hit a woman in the face. . . ."

"You imagined it, Maxim Menandrovich," she said almost cheerfully. "He didn't hit me in the face. He is an extremely refined person. And really, don't attach any importance to this episode. I have no need even to ask you to keep this to yourself, for I know that you have an old-fashioned nobility. But I do ask that you not think such a thing, even to yourself. The whole thing was nothing, very trivial. I would tell you about it, but there's nothing to tell."

"I'm not asking about anything."

"Of course, of course. But believe me, it's the kind of story that's impossible to tell coherently. It will always be comprehensible only to the participants. I would even like to share it with you—I trust you absolutely—but please don't be angry. There's nothing to tell."

She stopped and took out a mirror from the bag that swung from her shoulder.

"Wait a moment, I'll have a look. Please turn away for a second. There. Finished. I'm ready."

Bakhtin turned back. She had powdered her face, combed her hair, and applied lipstick to her lips.

"Shall we go?"

"Let's go."

When they walked up to the house, Fyodor Mikhailovich was looking out of the window at them.

* * *

A few days later, when Fyodor Mikhailovich, as usual, came running with the teapot in his hands and with his remark concerning the extraordinary energy efficiency of gas and the necessity never to leave it on, Bakhtin proposed that they drink tea together. The old man immediately agreed and sat down at the table in Maxim's half.

"I've noticed," he said, even before Maxim had filled his teacup, "that you are always looking at Lyudmila Grigoriyevna. Now don't be embarrassed—you are here without a woman—it's a fact of life. Only I would advise you not to. No, don't think it's because she's the wife of my son, but rather—how to put it—she's a bit unstable. This isn't her first marriage, and here in the village, I know they talk about her liaisons."

"Why are you telling me this, Fyodor Mikhailovich? There's no reason for me to know about this."

"And why not? There's no call for that here. You could gather this information from any source you please, from any neighbor, for example. And if you had a romance, I understand, it wouldn't be chivalrous to know about the woman's past—not even from her herself. But in this case?"

"Forgive me, Fyodor Mikhailovich, but even in my situation I have no business knowing about Lyudmila Grigoriyevna's past."

"That's the kind of nuance I don't comprehend, begging your pardon, although I seem to remember in my youth that I made a study of manners, yes sir."

"If you prefer, take it as my extravagance and not etiquette."

"Extravagance is the etiquette of old Russian literature," Fyodor Mikhailovich said, suddenly giving out a thin laugh.

"What?" Bakhtin asked, surprised.

"It's just something that I happened to remember. It's a term used by Professor Likhachev, isn't it?"

Maxim was silent. A strange conversation, a weird coda. But he couldn't help uttering something even stranger to himself: "The energy efficiency of literature is the etiquette of gas leakage." And he added, "A term used by Bakhtin. From his book *Amusing Literary Scholarship*."

"All right," Fyodor Mikhailovich said. "Enough of that. How do you find Lyova?"

"A fine, smart boy."

"How about without the hypocrisy, okay?"

"I'm not being a bit hypocritical. I said what I think."

"Really? I think he's a nasty boy. I've had no luck with my posterity, not with my son, not with my grandson. They're sort of gray, lackluster, and bad, emotionless. Especially Lev Nikolayevich. At times I have the feeling that he simply hates me."

"You are mistaken," Maxim replied drily, "in both cases, that is, with your son and with your grandson. As far as Lyova is concerned, I repeat, he seems to me to be a thoughtful, even talented child. He will yet come into his own, mark my words. In his relation with you he is truly complicated, but such is the style of your family, is it not? And besides, children of Lev's age always occasionally get to the point of hating their elders. There's nothing unnatural about that. It's simply the reverse side of their closeness to their loved ones."

"You suppose so?" the old man said thoughtfully. "But still, I think he's a horse's ass," he concluded cheerfully.

And Maxim understood that this tea time, which had been unpleasant for him, could be considered at an end. When Fyodor Mikhailovich went out, Bakhtin, after looking in all directions, took a full spoonful of jam and placed it on his tongue. There was a terribly bitter taste in his mouth, like during his childhood after a medicinal powder that was necessary to take with jam and to wash down with tea.

*   *   *

The August day had been exhaustingly hot, and a sultry night had begun. Maxim was covered with perspiration, but he was shivering. He trembled and crawled under the blanket. Under the blanket it became unendurable. He threw it off and began to shiver. Then he covered himself again, and again felt exhausted. Sleep did not come. In Maxim's head, someone turned on a record player and was uninterruptedly playing on it songs of Soviet composers: "And I will become yours completely, even without you"—"Not that icy blue . . . but green, green grass"—"And all your caring, like an iceberg in the ocean." It's cold. It's cold. It's hot. But this is boiled water, icy boiled water. It's boiling. Liquid oxygen is boiling, like an iceberg in the ocean, even without you. You are the shadow of shadows. I won't name you. Your face is cold and wicked. No, you are the green,

green grass. I'm going to hit you. I'm going to right now. It will be very painful. But forgive me, it's necessary. It hurts me, too. We'll endure it. And you forgive me, too. Not I. Not you. I'm alone. I want to be alone. I'll break loose. I will. There it is—thunder. It's thunder. Finally a thunderstorm, and a voice from the thunder. It's soft. I can't make it out. Pay attention. What is it?

"Maxim Menandrovich!"

"Ah, yes! Who's there?"

"Maxim Menandrovich, it's I, Fyodor Mikhailovich, look over here." The old man rapped on the window and, after receiving a look of recognition from Bakhtin, explained:

"You are evidently sick, you tossed and turned all night, I heard through the wall. Please forgive us, but Lyovushka and I can't be catching anything. We won't come into your room, but Lyovushka is going to place on the porch some warm milk and a sandwich. Take it and eat."

"Thank you, don't worry, I'll manage."

"Do you have medicine?"

"Yes, yes, thank you."

Maxim fell asleep again, without getting up from the bed and taking the milk. He heard himself cry out in his sleep, and he understood that he was delirious. He spoke very rapidly, sometimes swallowing his words, and sometimes speaking them extraordinarily distinctly. He lifted his right arm and brought it down with force on the bed. There was something he wanted, that he passionately desired, that he was striving for. And he understood. He formulated it: Separateness. Separateness and non-merging. That's it. That's freedom. Exactly. And again. Exactly. And a pounding drumroll. Ah?

"Grandfather asked me to find out if we should call a doctor?"

"Ah? No, thank you. I'll be okay. Thanks. It's better already. Thank you, thank you."

"Mother's coming tomorrow, she'll help, probably.

"Tomorrow? Can tomorrow be Saturday?"

"Yes."

"Aren't you mistaken? Tomorrow's Thursday."

"No, Saturday. You've already been sick for three days."

"Three days?"

"That's right."

Maxim stood up. He was swaying. His head was spinning. But he knew that his illness was subsiding. Apparently his elevated temperature had lasted for the entire three days. Now it was falling. There was a weakness. He asked Lyovushka for some strong tea, and he went out onto the porch after him. In the refrigerator there was a piece of cheese, and some bread rusks were found to go with the tea. Maxim ate it all, then lay down a bit, then stood up again and requested of himself to regain his health completely by the next day.

When on Saturday Lyudmila Grigoriyevna knocked on his door, Bakhtin, having been made anxious by Fyodor Mikhailovich's account, was already dressed and clean shaven. The bed was made. A much thinner Maxim smiled. In his hands he held a bag—he had to stock up on some provisions.

"So what's all this?" Lyudmila Grigoriyevna protested. "I'm not allowing you to go anywhere, you still have to lie down, and for two days or so I will somehow feed you." She left to putter in the kitchen, and Fyodor Mikhailovich came up to the window. After asking about his health, Fyodor Mikhailovich announced that he had some questions. Bakhtin proposed that he come in, supposing that his contagious period was past, but the grandfather declined the invitation, saying that he would be cautious for another two days. He asked his questions, standing by the window.

"Could you please explain what "inotapa" is, if I remember the word correctly."

"Inotapa? I don't know. What language is it?"

"Perhaps it's inopata?"

"That I don't know either. Why do you ask?"

"And another. I made a note: 'Relamarinia.'"

"Rella Manerinia?"

"Right, right!"

"Then everything's clear. I know the first word, too—it's inapatua."

"Correct. What is it?"

"Are you interested in Australian mythology, Fyodor Mikhailo-vich?"

"Not at all."

"But that's actually where those words are from."

"Explain their meaning, if you can, and then I'll tell you how and when I heard them."

"According to the notions of various Australian tribes, at the very beginning, when the whole earth was covered by the sea and only the highest peaks protruded from under the water, on the heights of these peaks there appeared 'glued people,'—rella manerinia, or inapatua. It was something like human embryos gathered into a lump, similar to linked larva. The glued embryos, with eyes, ears, and mouths closed, stirred about helplessly on the peaks until a certain ancestor reptile came from the north and with a knife separated the fetuses one from another, and with the same knife cut and trimmed their eyes, mouth, and ears. In other words, he gave them their final human appearance, after which he taught them everything that people have to know and to be able to do."

"Curious."

"Now it is your turn, Fyodor Mikhailovich, to satisfy my curiosity."

"You see, Maxim Menandrovich, the last two nights you often cried out and said those very words, which I wrote down as I heard them. I then decided to take an interest in them. Thank you for the valuable information."

"So that's what it was about," Maxim muttered and fell into thought, having discourteously forgotten about Fyodor Mikhailovich. The latter hovered at the window for a time, evidently wishing to continue the questioning, but noticing that Bakhtin had retired into his room, he reluctantly withdrew.

"Yes, yes," Maxim remembered, "that's exactly what I saw, 'glued people.' Oh God, and I was welded to the others in one lump. At the sides I had grown together with Nikolai Fyodorovich and Lyudmila Grigoriyevna, my head was stuck to that of Fyodor Mikhailovich, and my feet were attached to Lev Nikolayevich. There also were some people I didn't recognize; I don't remember. So there it is, this delirium and this nightmare—rella manerinia! Oh, what a nightmare!" Bakhtin winced, and his whole body started to ache in a strange way that he had never experienced before, around the edges.

Lyudmila Grigoriyevna brought his dinner on a tray.

"Today after dinner a short walk will be permitted," she said, smiling. "With a lady," she added coquettishly.

Maxim thanked her. He had actually been planning to walk a bit and indeed had wanted to ask Lyudmila Grigoriyevna to keep him company. She took his arm and they slowly walked to the river.

"I heard that you were telling Fyodor Mikhailovich about human larva, is that right? Did you have a dream? Or is it forbidden to ask about that?"

"No, why ever not? It's just that I still don't remember everything. But it seems to me it was the most terrifying dream of my life."

"How so?"

"In my dream I felt myself undifferentiated from a multiplicity of people, who were strangers to me. All together, we were a swarming helpless mass with a common, but rather benighted, consciousness. Some sort of thoughts raced around in my head, individual ones but unclear and unintelligible. I wanted to turn around, but I could not. Then somehow or other my right hand got free and after a time a Finnish knife appeared in it. Individual consciousness awakened, and I understood that it was necessary for me to cut my way out of the general mass, that is, to cut my way out literally: to cut out my body the way they use a coping saw to cut out a figure from the middle of a piece of plywood. And yet that's not a good analogy—plywood is homogeneous, but we glued people each had our own form. I had to use the Finka to strike around the edges. I struck—and I cut into living flesh. To the right of me was a woman. I had to separate myself from her, first of all. She howled. It was painful. I, too, wailed and asked her forgiveness, explaining that it would be better this way and that it was necessary. We lay in our blood, and I struck and struck and struck again around the edges.

Bakhtin waved his hand to show how he wielded the knife, and Lyudmila Grigoriyevna looked at him with fright.

"How horrible!" she said.

"Yes. I remember that even then, in delirium, I was able to formulate the idea of freedom and the right of non-merging and of being separate. And I consider that an achievement, since the hardest thing of all was to separate my head, into which thoughts from a nearby stranger's head were persistently flowing. I have to admit that those foreign thoughts somehow acquired authoritative distinctness and persistence. However, I have forgotten those foreign thoughts utterly."

"That was Fyodor Mikhailovich?" Lyudmila Grigoriyevna asked quietly. "That is, I mean the stranger's head with authoritative thoughts. Was that him? All right, don't answer, I know already. I even guessed the woman."

"Yes?" Maxim said, surprised.

"By the way, you really do sleep head to head—the same wall is at your headboard. As far as his authoritativeness and strength go, you should have met him ten years ago. What a man he was!"

Curiosity awakened in Bakhtin, but he was silent, waiting for Lyudmila Grigoriyevna herself to begin to speak. He was not mistaken. She evidently wished to talk about this.

"The Domostroi[5] was always sufficient for this family, and Fyodor Mikhailovich was absolute ruler and despot in it. Only one person on rare occasions dared to stage a mild revolt. That was the oldest son, Yuri Fyodorovich. He died fifteen years ago."

She gave her shoulders a shake, as if from cold, and fell into thought.

"He died quite young and without evident cause. He was a talented person, but very sad. I mean, I wanted to tell you about Fyodor Mikhailovich. . . ."

"Yes?"

"He took his daughter-in-law away from his son. There. And Fyodor Mikhailovich, therefore. . . . Such was the conqueror's strength in him, that a woman who was then still quite young . . . without thinking . . . without shame . . . proudly looking people in the eye. . . . And Yuri Fyodorovich. . . . No, forgive me. It seems I overestimated my strength."

Lyudmila Grigoriyevna found her kerchief, wiped her eyes, and blew her nose. They had reached the river and had stopped.

"You shouldn't stay here," she said. "You are still not completely well, and your first walk has dragged on. Let's go back."

"Let's go," Maxim agreed. He was truly very tired—whether from the walk or from the conversation, God only knew.

* * *

The first desire that arose in Bakhtin as soon as he recovered from his illness was to set about writing his article. This had happened to him before. Ill health in some mysterious way provided a stimu-

---

5. *Translator's note*: The Domostroi was a 16th-century compendium of household rules and religious prescriptions that was to govern Russian family life, known for prescribing total power to the husband, even sanctioning his violence against other family members.

lus to work that had seemed to be at a dead end. It was as if a creative crisis had been overcome, together with, and by means of, a physical one. Bakhtin sensed that some sort of subterranean shift had occurred; some sort of mixing had occurred in consciousness, both in his opinions and in his very intentions. Maxim coldly looked over his notes again. Nothing was right, nothing: character, fleshing out, the other, the double, transgredience, embryo. Embryo? Embryo! Yes, embryo. A lump of glued embryos. Glued people—rella manerinia. That's it! Not doubles, but linked human larva, with dim thoughts, unopened eyes, and locked-shut mouths. Monologism? It's nothing but common consciousness. Dialogism? What is that, except complete undifferentiation. How did people obtain completion? They were separated one from the other, they were torn apart, they were cut off, their barely noticeable nostrils, slits of eyes, and mouths were cut through with a knife. And who did this? The ancestor lizard. And what is more like an embryo than a lizard? It is an embryo—the first one to separate itself successfully from the glued human larva. There he is—the author—the ancestor lizard. And there's his first gesture, to cut along the edges with a Finnish knife. To free himself and his own: to open eyes, ears, nostrils, and mouths. And the author stands there, covered with blood—his own and others'. No, others' blood is not correct. The blood is his and not his. Here exists a simultaneity of properties: his and not his at the same time, all one blood. The author directs his speech at a character, and the character answers in his own words. His own or the author's? Does the author know what the character will answer? He knows and doesn't know, and the words are the author's and the character's, his and not his. There is no freedom greater than an author's, and no greater unfreedom, too. Rella manerinia! Bakhtin noted down these words as terms in poetics, and following the custom of recent literary scholarship, encoded it with an abbreviation: R.M. He now intended to make those letters the title of his article. However, the more Bakhtin thought about R.M., the more clearly he understood that that sort of scholarly article could not be written. If they would perhaps criticize "transgredience" as a non-Russian word, what of R.M.? No, of course, it's not a question of the title. An Australian term at the present time is no more foreign than Greek or Latin. It's a question of method. Bakhtin was not able to explain his discovery in scholarly terms. Indeed, from the very beginning, no matter how he cloaked his subject in terms such as "prototype," "transposition," and "laws of translation," Maxim's endeavor went beyond scholarship.

"But M. M. Bakhtin," Bakhtin thought with vexation, "concealed clearly nonscholary scholarly material behind his 'transgredience'! However, M. M. clearly conceived of his work as higher than poetics, and even art."

Maxim's ambitions were, of course, more modest. But did they reach the sphere of art, did they entirely leave the area of theory? Bakhtin wrote:

"A prototype, it goes without saying, is assimilated by the author, but its metamorphosis, accompanied by renaming the prototype as the character, occurs through a dual process of familial joining with the author and alienation from him, regardless of the artistic system—monological or dialogical—it takes place in."

Stepping away from his writing, Bakhtin took a clean sheet of paper:

"A large drop of blood, fresh as dew, pleasing to the eye with the succulence of its color, fell from Bakhtin's breast onto the gray head of Fyodor Mikhailovich.

'The pain, my God, what pain!' said the old man. 'My grandson, Lev Nikolayevich, is a kleptomaniac!'"

The sheets of paper lay side by side.

"So, what now?" Bakhtin thought. "Who here has become the character? Fyodor Mikhailovich? Bakhtin? And if he has become it, then how? Banalities. Both versions are banal!" he decided, and crumpled both sheets of paper.

* * *

At one point on a Sunday, when all the Pavlovs were assembled, Bakhtin heard excited voices coming from the owners' side. He recognized the precise speech of Fyodor Mikhailovich and the angry rapid-fire of Nikolai Fyodorovich.

"How many times have I asked you not to meddle!"

"I am not meddling, but I had to warn you. Are you my son or are you not my son?"

"Father, I am quite of an age where that no longer has any meaning."

"It always has meaning."

"And I say, don't meddle."

"And I say, it's she, Lyuska, who is egging you on, and I have to tell you that she . . . ," but his voice faded to a whisper.

"A bad lot! You are nothing but a bad lot, Father!"

"How dare you? To your father? Try it again—and I'll alter your physiognomy, understand? Milksop! You just ask her, ask her yourself, you son of a bitch! Lyuska is yours!"

"Stop it."

"I won't even consider it. I'll tell you another thing . . . ," but again the conversation became inaudible.

"What?!"

"Yes."

"It's a lie."

"Check it yourself!"

Bakhtin saw Nikolai Fyodorovich dart out of the house and head toward the summer kitchen, where Lyudmila Grigoriyevna was puttering around. Upon entering, he closed the door behind him. Their conversation was not audible, although from time to time cries could be heard from that direction.

"It was he? He said that?" Lyudmila Grigoriyevna howled. "And you believed him? Whose words are those? Is it you who's talking?"

"The last time!" he shouted. "You! I'll tell you who you are!"

"It's I. I am talking. He's your father! Don't you dare say that about your father! Don't forget yourself!"

The kitchen door swung open and was violently slammed behind Lyudmila Grigoriyevna. Weeping, she ran to the gate. Tearing off her apron on the run, she threw it onto the gooseberry bushes. She disappeared. Nikolai Fyodorovich emerged from the kitchen with a measured gait, glanced at Bakhtin's window, picked up the apron, carried it into the kitchen, and returned to the house.

"So now what?" Fyodor Mikhailovich asked.

"Nothing," Nikolai Fyodorovich answered.

"Are you convinced?"

"Get lost, disgusting old man!"

The grandfather wailed like an animal.

Under Maxim's window, someone was quietly laughing. Bakhtin looked out. Pressed to the wall and twisted up, Lev Nikolayevich was pleased about something.

That day, Lyudmila Grigoriyevna did not appear again at the house. The next morning, Nikolai Fyodorovich left for work. In the evening, as Bakhtin was working on the veranda, he suddenly saw the door open and Lyudmila Grigoriyevna appear in the entryway. Placing her finger to her lips, she quickly went to the light switch and clicked it off.

"I ask you, please don't turn the light on," she said. "I don't want anyone to see me."

Maxim silently sat her down at the table next to himself.

"Give me your hand," she whispered, and took Bakhtin by the hand.

He felt moisture on his palms—the combined moisture of tears and kisses. A man in such a situation will always attempt to pull his hand back, but that would be wrong, he shouldn't. Maxim understood this and did not withdraw his hand.

"Thank you, Maxim Menandrovich. You . . . you know, I can't, I can't go on. . . . I can't go on any . . . more. . . ."

She plunged her head in his lap and burst into sobs. He stroked her hair. She seized his hand again and began to cover it with kisses.

"What's wrong," he said. "What's wrong, Lyu—(it was strange now to call her Lyudmila Grigoriyevna)—what's wrong, Lyuda?"

"Lyusya," she said. "Not Lyuda, you hear? Lyusya! Say it, Lyusya!"

"Lyusya," he uttered.

"Good. Now say something else."

"What should I say?"

"Say anything at all. Please!"

"I don't know."

"Do you feel contempt for me?"

"I? Heaven forbid!"

"I'm a bad lot, with no morals, but it's he, he made me this way. No, no, it's me. I myself am guilty. But what is to be done? I can't, I can't be different. So, say something!"

"Everything will be all right," Bakhtin said, stupidly.

"Do you think so?"

"Of course."

"And you aren't angry that I came to you?"

"What's to be angry about?"

"And everything will be all right with us?"

"It will."

"I am afraid that Fyodor Mikhailovich might hear us."

"From the veranda nothing is audible," Maxim said reassuringly.

"Dummy." "We're not staying on the veranda," she said, smiling.

Bakhtin did not immediately know what to answer, but he quickly agreed with this estimate of his intellect. Such a turn of events he had not expected, and certainly had not wished for.

"How can this be?" he thought, but he remembered that some literary character or other—who?—had affirmed that there is no greater sin than to refuse a woman.

"We'll be quiet," he managed to say.

"Can you do it quietly? I can't." Lyusya burst out laughing.

"Then the landlords will turn me out tomorrow promptly. In the lease it's agreed that there be no overnight guests, no women."

"Oh, I know, the landlady is especially strict on that point. But maybe Fyodor Mikhailovich will put in a good word."

"I don't think he'll miss the slightest word."

They went into the room noiselessly. Bakhtin in the darkness looked on as Lyudmila Grigoriyevna undressed, and God knows what his head was occupied with. Mephistopheles asked him:

And do you know, my philosopher,
What you were thinking at that time,
When no one thinks?
Can you say?

No, Bakhtin did not want Mephistopheles to talk about that.

"Come here, my dear, come," she said, using only her lips with no voice.

He approached, cold, pensive, gloomy.

"Don't be sad," she said.

Constraint held him back, but Lyusya did not let that bother her. She became the Bacchante, and Maxim ceased to be differentiated from all others. During that time when no one thinks, thoughts evaporated from his head as well.

At five in the morning, she got up so as to leave on the train un-noticed. Bakhtin saw her to the station.

"What happens now?" he thought.

"Don't be nervous." Lyudmila Grigoriyevna laughed, guessing at his anxiety. "I paid for everything in advance. So even if the old man heard something, it won't help him at all. You can't pay for the same crime twice."

Maxim did not understand anything.

"Yes, and what do you think that scandal was about two days ago?"

"How should I know?"

"You see, the recent scandal took place because of what happened only this past night."

"How can that be?" Bakhtin said, surprised.

"Simple, my dear," Lyusya said cheerfully. "Fyodor Mikhailovich so distinctly foresaw our relationship, that for him it had already become real before it was a reality. He even told Kolya about it as if it were something that had already happened."

"A kind of delirium!"

"Delirium? Not entirely delirium. And you know, I am grateful to him. Without that, I perhaps would not have come over to you, and you . . . you are, in my opinion, a slow-witted person! Yes?" She reached up and met his lips with hers.

The train approached.

"Don't be sad," Lyusya said, and waved her hand.

Bakhtin walked a bit in the forest and returned to the house around six. Fyodor Mikhailovich was already up. He gazed at Bakhtin penetratingly and asked:

"Insomnia? I heard you toss and turn all night."

"Sorry," Maxim said. "I probably disturbed you."

"For me, you see, there's no getting used to it. It's been a long time since I slept at night. So don't apologize. But is something bothering you?"

"Work isn't going well," Bakhtin said, with a genuine sigh.

"That's nothing. It'll come around."

* * *

"Maxim Menandrovich," Nikolai Fyodorovich called out some time later. "Will you help me? Our water tank is broken."

"With pleasure, but I'm not very handy."

"Skill is not required. You only have to justify your patronymic. Masculine strength is needed. Did I remember the meaning of your patronymic correctly?"

"Absolutely right."

"So there. Agreed?"

"I'm ready."

They left. Bakhtin's help was basically unnecessary—from time to time he simply applied pressure to some tool or other.

"I've been wanting to ask you, Maxim Menandrovich. It seems you don't respect Lyudmila Grigoriyevna very much?"

"That will do, Nikolai Fyodorovich. Can I have given you the slightest grounds for your question?"

"Well, we aren't exactly blind. Even father also noticed."

"Fyodor Mikhailovich himself said this to you?"

"Yes, he and I had a talk."

"That's strange. I must assure you that that absolutely does not correspond to the truth. I have nothing but the most genuine esteem for Lyudmila Grigoriyevna. Moreover, I am obliged to her by gratitude for her countless attentions to me—regarding my health, my appetite, even my work. And how else am I supposed to relate to her? I can't imagine—what blunder did I commit that allows you to suppose what you are supposing? Is it possible that I was guilty of some incivility? Point it out to me, or else I will start to feel very uncomfortable."

"Please don't be distressed, Maxim Menandrovich. I am not reprimanding you. Understand me correctly. It's just that rumors are going around the village. They may have reached you."

"I haven't heard anything, and if I had, it wouldn't affect our relations."

"Lyudmila Grigoriyevna has had a lot of pain. She's been through a lot. Her first husband died quite young, and she was shattered by that."

"Did you know him?" asked Bakhtin, surprising himself in altering his custom of not asking intimate questions of distant acquaintances.

"Did I know him? Um, in a certain sense, I knew him well. He was my older brother."

He remembered: Yuri Fyodorovich—smart fellow—a rebel—a seducer of a daughter-in-law.

"And I fell in love with Lyudmila Grigoriyevna the very minute Yuri brought her into our house."

"Forgive me, Nikolai Fyodorovich," Maxim said with emphasis. "It's not I but you who are showing disrespect to Lyudmila Grigoriyevna!"

"You think so?" Nikolai Fyodorovich said thoughtfully, tightening the nut on the water tank forcefully. "Well anyway, time flies, our marriage is already fifteen years old. No short service. Love dies— you see the person differently, you get irritated, and so forth." His lips parted in an eerie grin, but in his eyes flashed something resembling helplessness.

"My God, he loves her terribly," it dawned on Bakhtin. "And Fyodor Mikhailovich . . . he too . . . he loves her too. Brother-competitors. Father-seducer of a daughter-in-law. And now also my story with her."

* * *

"Lyovushka," Bakhtin said the next day. "I'm leaving the house soon, and I wanted to give you a little present. Do you remember, on the day I moved in, that I gave you an assignation from 1860? Now to improve your collection, here's a coin from the same time."

"Thanks for the coin, but I don't have the assignation any more."

"Why not? Did you exchange it for something?"

"No, I didn't. Grandfather took it away."

"Took it away? Why?"

"He heard you say that that woman burned money like that—what was her name?"

"Nastasya Filippovna"

"Right. So you see."

"See what?"

"You see, he took it away and burned it."

"Burned it? Whatever for?"

"He said it was to see what she, that Nastasia Filippovna, saw."

"For that, he should have burned the money I gave him as rent for the summer house," Bakhtin muttered.

"Do you think I could come see you in Moscow?" Lyova asked.

"Of course, Lyovushka, do come, I'll be glad to see you. Here's my address and telephone number," Maxim said, embracing the boy. The latter reached up and kissed Maxim.

That evening Fyodor Mikhailovich summoned Bakhtin:

"I heard you're getting ready to leave."

"Yes, I've already ordered a car."

"What is this leaving before the time is up? You might stay a bit longer."

"Things to do," Maxim answered briefly.

"Your decision, your decision. However, even though you are leaving early, there are a few unsettled accounts."

"Yes, yes, of course."

"Here's a little list."

"Could we do without the list?"

"No, why? This is for gas, this is for electricity, and this is for the broken window."

"The window?" said Bakhtin with surprise.

"Yes indeed, it evidently slipped your mind, but Lev Nikolayevich was telling me that you broke it. Or was he lying?"

Maxim looked for the boy. He was quietly standing on the porch.

"Ah, yes, yes, I remember, forgive me. It's the honest truth. I broke it. I should have told you about it myself. Please try to forgive me. Here."

"Well, that's the complete accounting. The matter is closed, and, I hope, to our mutual satisfaction."

"Completely," Bakhtin affirmed, and went out into his half. He waited for Lyovushka to come and explain about the window, but he did not come. Rather, in the final days before Maxim's departure, the boy avoided him.

On Saturday, when the car arrived, all the Pavlovs assembled. Maxim, weighed down by his things, came to say good-bye. The men were gathered on the porch, and it occurred to Bakhtin that he was seeing them for the first time together marshaled in a row. He cast his glance from one to the other, and a strange feeling seized him. It seemed he was looking at a picture as in the detective movies with artists' renderings of criminals. Except that in the movies, the eyes move and change, but here, although the eyes also darted about, they nevertheless moved from face to face—without changing. They were the same green, mournful eyes. But still and all, it seemed to Bakhtin that the eyes were predominantly at the disposal of Fyodor Mikhailovich and that his melancholy overflowed with moisture in those eyes.

"Ah, old man, old man," Bakhtin sighed. "What fruit have you brought forth on this earth? What have you wrought! And where did you put Lyusya, you unbearable people?"

As if hearing these words, the grandfather squinted in the direction of the kitchen. There, leaning against the doorpost, stood Lyudmila Grigoriyevna. She took off her apron and slowly waved her hand.

"Good-bye," Bakhtin said. "Remember me kindly."

"Good-bye, Maxim Menandrovich!"

"All the best!" (This was from Lyudmila Grigoriyevna.)

He thinks he has fought his way out. Yes, he dashed off to Moscow. May God go with him. His obsessive idea was: differentiation and non-merging. But tell me, my friend, where exactly do you see the author in all of this? Of course, you think it's Bakhtin—who else? But Bakhtin himself clearly said, "I am a literary scholar, a simple literary scholar." And the truth is that wherever he is, the only thing he can do is R.M. So now, dear friend, you'll begin to think that the author is Fyodor Mikhailovich. But you'll be mistaken. Then you'll say, Who the devil else? The author is the one who wrote all of this. No, no, no! Not me at all. That is to say, it was I, of course, but who is this I? In any case, I for one don't know. It's not for me to know. See you later. Remember: "Rella manerinia."

Autumn 1985–February 1986

TRANSLATOR'S AFTERWORD

A PARODY OF FREUD

On one level, "The Rehabilitation of Freud" is a parody of Freudian ideas. Volodya's over-the-top Oedipus complex comes complete with sexual dreams about his mother and elaborate plans for an incestuous involvement with his mother-in-law. External events occur in a dream-like but obvious way to underline a psychological point (Volodya's beating; the death of his mother; the snapping shut of the mouse-trap). A murderous wish is brought into hallucinogenic juxtaposition with a corresponding death. The story races through the events of Volodya's young adulthood concentrating on his all-too-obvious oe-dipal problems. The tone is generally light, and many passages are humorous—until the very last paragraph, when the hero's sudden death destroys the equanimity of the narrator, who suddenly ques-tions what he has been doing telling this story. The story is thus a parody that gets out of hand, but in so doing indicates something star-tlingly serious about its subject. Against the background of Soviet intellectual chitchat about the newly fashionable Freud, Beilis wrote an amusing parody that ends in a horrifying sudden death.

In addition to parodying the fashionable Freud and hinting at the seriousness of Freud's ideas, however, Beilis also placed in the title several ironies for the Soviet reader. First, the word "rehabilitation" evoked for Soviet ears the entire process of de-Stalinization, in which many thousands of people were "rehabilitated" from their previous "repression." These two terms were weasel words, chosen by the post-Stalin political elite to permit them officially to admit Stalin's crimes while largely maintaining the system he had constructed. "Repression" in the post-Stalin lexicon could mean any level of unjust treatment at the hands of the regime, ranging from the loss of a job to loss of freedom to loss of life. The word "rehabilitation" had a correspondingly wide lexical meaning, ranging from reinstatement at work to release from prison to posthumous vindication of innocence. Against the background of these multifarious Soviet "rehabilitations," the notion of Freud's rehabilitation represented a first layer of irony for the readers of this story.

The deeper irony implied in the title lay in the juxtaposition of Volodya's infatuation with Freud coupled with his own demise. The doctor may be rehabilitated, but the patient dies. If the hero, with his feverish infatuation with Freud and his other intellectual efforts, could not save himself from being crushed by his demons, then just what does Freud's rehabilitation mean? The narrator himself loses his composure at the very end of the story, faced with recounting the shocking end of Volodya's life. That breakdown also signals the collapse of parodic distance to the subject. What started as a humorous exploration ends by overwhelming both the narrator and the reader with its sadness. Clearly something is touched on in the story that surpasses parody.

VOLODYA'S STRUGGLE

Volodya's sudden death affects us in part because we are drawn to the intelligence, seriousness, and resourcefulness he brings to the task of trying to become psychologically healthy. We are moved by his struggle to overcome his sexual difficulties all the more because he is so successful—but always only to a point. At each stage, Beilis lets us see that some part of the puzzle of his inner life always eludes him.

He has a date with a young woman, but he does not know how to kiss. He is successful in kissing, but he cannot have pleasurable intercourse. He successfully manages intercourse, but the duration is insufficient and he doubts that the woman was satisfied. He successfully manages protracted intercourse, but his mother dies, setting in motion a series of paranoid and self-destructive thoughts. He achieves a relationship that combines passionate love and rapturous sex, but his work falls apart and he feels dead inside. And finally, he becomes a father, but before he can take his newborn daughter in his arms, he inadvertently steps in front of an oncoming truck.

In addition, in situation after situation, we see Volodya undermine himself after a sexual success. When Irina slips away after their first encounter, Volodya's mind quickly begins to eviscerate his feeling of miraculous achievement (his first successful sexual intercourse). In succession, he thinks: the act was a mere trick played on him; she had planned everything in advance; and she must have been dissatisfied with the brevity of the intercourse. Instead of basking in the glow of his recent triumph, Volodya discounts it, plagued with thoughts of Irina's premeditation and dissatisfaction.

After the death of his mother (which comes immediately after his second encounter with Irina), his thoughts turn against himself with particular ferocity. Through a complicated series of reasonings, in which he views Irina as the symbolic murderer both of Volodya's mentrix at the institute and of the image of Volodya's mother in him, Volodya arrives at the conclusion that, somehow through the instrumentality of Irina, he is responsible for his mother's death. He is thus not able to separate the events in his life from events in the life of his mother. In both of these cases, Irina's unexpected departure and his mother's unexpected death, we see a flood of angry guilt feelings welling up in Volodya.

This guilt, which is lodged deeper in Volodya's mind than he can conceive, must be seen as responsible for the final two misfortunes of Volodya's life, which are otherwise inexplicable: the inner deadness that accompanies his conjugal bliss with Natasha, and his accidental death. Again and again, Volodya thinks he has taken the measure of his difficulty and has emerged victorious, but he is mistaken every time. Whatever the original parodic intent of the story, the rehabilitation of Freud also means learning how far out of touch our consciousness can be with our deeper feelings.

VOLODYA'S READING

During his university years, after a string of unsuccessful encounters with young women, Volodya turns to Freud for relief and self-understanding. His initial reaction to Freud's ideas is "feverish" as he "applied everything to himself, and everything fit." By this point in the story, we have been told enough to understand his feverish response. Volodya has had conscious fantasies and regular nocturnal dreams in which he has defeated his stepfather for the sexual attentions of his mother—which he then proceeds to enjoy in the most explicit manner. No wonder the phrase "Oedipus complex" sends a shiver through him when he first hears it. With such undisguised oedipal dreams and fantasies, Volodya clearly needs no persuading that the Oedipus complex is the keystone of male psychology.

He wants relief from his crippling inability to interact satisfyingly with young women. When he tries to kiss a woman, his incestuous dream life is activated, causing him to close his eyes and remove himself emotionally from the woman—who in each case is repulsed by his behavior. We might note that the negative feelings in Volodya to which all of his women friends react ultimately derive from the same guilt that ruins his happiness and pleasure throughout the story. This piece of the puzzle seems to elude him. In his mind, he sees a clear link between his sexual problems and his feelings for his mother, and then expects cure to result from this insight. But although his unconscious libidinal life is indeed known to him, his aggression and the guilt that it fuels are not. His reading of Freud puts him in touch only with the part that is already available to him.

And yet Freud's theory does give Volodya "hope." He plans to fall in love with his mother-in-law. He takes this from Freud's idea of the unconscious incestuous currents between mothers-in-law and sons-in-law, as outlined primarily in *Totem and Taboo*. He will find a mother-in-law who, within a normal, respectable relationship, will somehow be able to give him the erotic pleasures he has had from his dreams. Like all of Volodya's attempts to recover from his crippling illness, this one shows resourcefulness, intelligence, and some insight. He aims to neutralize his incestuous dream life by investing in his mother-in-law the energy that is generating his incestuous dreams, and thereby to render his relationship with her daughter a normal one. So he sets out to fall in love with a mother whom he can convert into a mother-in-law. He visits his female friends in their homes to get a look at their mothers, but the plan fails. He feels no desire for any of the mothers. At this point, he abandons his plan and rejects Freud, calling his ideas "raving nonsense."

What, then, is Volodya's experience of reading Freud? First, there was feverish intellectual excitement at seeing his problems reflected so clearly in an important theory. When it became clear that the theory did not show the way to a solution, the excitement died away. Then Volodya turned to action. Both the feverish excitement and the plan of action indicate that Volodya sought a cure not through giving up his incestuous desires as unrealistic but by finding an acceptable way to satisfy them. He reads Freud so as to keep open the possibility of satisfying an incestuous desire by consciously displacing it onto a mother-in-law rather than by repressing and sublimating it. He turns what for Freud was a *theory* of the unconscious elements of an everyday relationship into a plan of *action*. If sublimation is the process by which instinctual drives are suppressed but given satisfaction in symbolic form, then Volodya's reading of Freud must be seen as a unique compromise moving in a direction away from sublimation. For his plan of finding a mother-in-law to fall in love with does not seem to be a plan to seduce his mother-in-law—which would be to undo sublimation entirely—but rather to find a mother-in-law to love with more ardor than is usually the case.

After his Freud-inspired action plan to secure the love of a mother-in-law fails, he takes a direct action not inspired by Freud: he "decides to get married." Soon after this, he speaks to Natasha on the street. Interestingly, from this first meeting with Natasha to both encounters with Irina (at least their beginnings) and finally to his fatal encounter with a truck, all the decisive moments in Volodya's life occur on the street. It is as if he can escape being dominated by his unconscious fantasies only by acting (or being acted upon) in the most public space there is. But although each of these actions leads to greater sexual fulfillment, they ultimately do not lead to happiness. Rather, they end in death. Despite his having overcome all his symptoms by the end of the story in the area of sexual dysfunction, he still has not dealt with his unconscious conflicts. His sexual objects stand in the shadow of his continuing unconscious incestuous fantasies, which, even if they no longer appear in his nocturnal dreams, continue to generate guilt and discomfort in his waking life.

Volodya, for his part, in the flush of his new relationship with Natasha, takes the measure of the evidence available to him and proclaims victory over Freud and his neurosis. His soon-to-be mother-in-law does not resemble his mother, and therefore, according to Freudian theory, "his marriage choice had not been based on his mother." When during the pre-wedding period he has no dreams,

Volodya optimistically concludes, "That's the end of it," supposing that he has solved his psychological problem. Unfortunately for him, when he attempts to do with Natasha in reality what he had previously done only in his incestuous dreams, he finds that he still needs "his vision, his delightful nightmare" even to simulate intercourse. Thus action has not removed the problem after all. It has simply driven it out of consciousness, beyond even his dreams.

The other occasion of Volodya's reading in the story concerns *Hamlet*. Once again, theory is made to serve the purposes of action. His long monologue on *Hamlet*, based on the oedipal interpretation of *Hamlet* first put forward by Freud and then elaborated on by Ernest Jones, is itself an action, designed to break a pattern of unsuccessful encounters with women. However, as in his reading of Freud, Volodya in reading *Hamlet* confuses unconscious and conscious motivation. According to him, instead of unconsciously desiring his mother (or the image of her from his early childhood), Hamlet does so consciously. Volodya sees Hamlet as having a *conscious* plan to "possess" his mother. In Volodya's retelling, everything else in the play is subordinate to this plan. Thus instead of Shakespeare's tragedy about a son's mysteriously postponed revenge of a father's murder, Volodya interprets the play as an incestuous love story, as if the only thing on Hamlet's mind was to sexually possess his mother. This interpretation, which Volodya later remembers reading in "some Freudian book or other," does nevertheless help Volodya achieve what he wants in action. It makes possible his first successful kiss.

VOLODYA AND ADULTHOOD

The fact that we are not given Volodya's patronymic and last name means that we are not permitted to view him in any way other than intimately, through his nickname, the name used by family and friends—and now by the author and by us. Had we been given his full complement of names, as we are in the case of virtually all major characters in the works of Tolstoy and Dostoyevsky, we would have had access to Volodya's experience in the adult, formal world in which Russians address each other by name and patronymic. For example, if Volodya's father had been named Ivan, Volodya would have been known in formal settings as Vladimir Ivanovich. In the course of the day at the research institute, he would have been often addressed in this formal manner. We are told the names and patronymics of his major coworkers, Anna Aleksandrovna and Irina Mikhailovna, but we know him only as Volodya.

This fact mirrors his inability to become an adult. The story, after all, covers those years in a man's life in which he takes on an adult identity and begins to act in the adult world. Although Volodya is a success in his job at the institute, Beilis shows us that in the deeper layers of his emotional life, he never sufficiently renounces his incestuous attachment to his mother so as to be free of the guilt associated with that attachment. By withholding Volodya's patronymic from us, Beilis highlights his character's entrapment in his infantile desire for his mother, the patronymic, of course, pointing back to the father. Interestingly, his death occurs at precisely the moment in which his first name has become the patronymic of his daughter. If she were called Svetlana, her formal name would be Svetlana Vladimirovna. Every Russian father takes joy in holding his newborn in his arms and addressing the infant with the formal name that he or she will bear many years later as an adult. Minutes before Volodya is to have this experience, he steps in front of a truck.

The key to Volodya's adulthood is the fact that he does not repress his incestuous feelings for his mother. As a teenager, at the beginning of the story, he experiences those feelings consciously. Later, he looks for a mother onto whom he can displace those feelings as her son-in-law. His reading excites him in part because it shows him that his preoccupations are shared, in literature and in psychoanalytic theory. Even after he begins his relationship with Natasha and continues his sexual education with Irina, he is prone to the irrational guilt feelings that indicate that he is still deeply involved with his mother, but unconsciously. When his mother dies on the same night as his supposedly final liberation from his sexual problems, he convinces himself that his session with Irina somehow caused his mother's death. He therefore feels that he is his mother's murderer. Such guilt points to a deep though unconscious incestuous bond. His accidental death must be seen as the ultimate price he pays for these irrational guilt feelings. Because he feels guilty for unconsciously desiring something that is prohibited, he cannot permit himself to enjoy his triumphs—we have seen this pattern throughout his life. At the moment of greatest triumph—the birth of his daughter—he must find a way to deny himself this final triumphant pleasure because of the guilt he continues to feel.

Volodya thus is a man who deals with his incestuous feelings for his mother using several defenses but *not* that of repression. Repression is defined as the mind's excluding certain thoughts and feelings from consciousness because they are felt to be so upsetting that they cannot be acknowledged as existing. Volodya is made uncomfortable by his explicit fantasies involving his mother and her husbands—they make his life difficult with his mother and stepfather—but he does not repress them. Here is Beilis's description of the way these fantasies stopped being conscious and started being part of his nocturnal dream life. These scenes "appeared again and again, changing form and developing. And they became his dreams; he no longer allowed them into consciousness. But dreams cannot be stopped—in fact, they can become more and more unruly." This may be a certain kind of denial, but it is not repression. Volodya's relation to his own fantasies can be taken as an explication of what Alexander Etkind meant when he said that Russians, living closer to their unconscious, are not as subject to repression as Westerners. Volodya's existence in contemporary Russian literature is not by itself proof of Etkind's statement. It is rather a precise exemplification of what Etkind was talking about—a Russian culture that is less built on repression than is the West European culture that formed the background to Freud's early works.

BAKHTIN AND THE PAVLOV FAMILY

When Bakhtin starts to get to know them, he feels that he has "entered into the system in regular operation in the Pavlov family, that he filled out a missing element in that system." One sense in which he fills out a missing element is comic: the literary scholar Bakhtin, who is not *the* M. M. Bakhtin, is coming to live with Fyodor Mikhailovich, who is not *the* Fyodor Mikhailovich Dostoyevsky, and Lev Nikolayevich, who is not *the* Lev Nikolayevich Tolstoy. The literarily named Pavlovs now have a Bakhtin among them (whose real counterpart's most famous book dealt with the poetics of Dostoyevsky). The system of their literary pretensions is now complete. As he comes to know them better, though, the comedy fades as Bakhtin learns that the Pavlovs are, as he says in parting, "unbearable people." Indeed they are scarcely people at all, if being a person is understood to denote having a self. For "the system in regular operation in the Pavlov family" denies selfhood to everyone except the eagle-nosed patriarch, Fyodor Mikhailovich—with selfhood understood to mean the capacity to act on one's own behalf.

We first see the operation of that system on the 13-year-old grandson, Lev Nikolayevich. His daily life is rigidly controlled by his grandfather, and he is imprisoned by his famous literary name and patronymic. The names of his son and grandson have already been picked, the progeny being thus already imprisoned before birth. He is an expert in false fronts, quickly involving Bakhtin in a cover story for the benefit of the ever-listening grandfather, to try to salvage some small amount of personal agency, even if illicitly. He is seething with an anger that he can express only in somnambulism and acts of petty crime. He best expresses his non-authentic sense of self in his hobby of drawing banknotes, thus creating amateur counterfeit money; and the portrait he draws on one banknote combines features of Dostoyevsky, his grandfather, and his own face. He clearly craves Bakhtin's affection and regard. Witness his excited reaction to the idea for a day trip and to the invitation to visit Bakhtin after the summer is over. Nevertheless, he resorts to the crudest manipulations to gain the older man's support (he leaves a stolen bicycle in Bakhtin's room, thus forcing him to become either an accomplice or a stool pigeon).

The portrait expresses Lev's profoundly confused identity. As he himself shouts out, his grandfather is his "repulsive double." And when the search for the stolen bicycle is at its height and the grandson is furious that he is being suspected of the theft, he shouts, "If you, Fyodor Mikhailovich, were a kleptomaniac in your youth, that does not mean that I am obliged to repeat your life experience with all your errors and flaws! I am not Fyodor Mikhailovich. I am Lev Nikolayevich!" The boy seems desperately to be trying to assert his own identity against a general suspiciousness—until we learn that he actually *did* steal the bicycle. He therefore *was* repeating his grandfather's early life (and apparently self-consciously), although we readers do not learn of the grandfather's "kleptomania" until later. Thus the repetition seems to have been undertaken in part to give the grandson the opportunity both to reenact his grandfather's crime and to decry the suspicion that he might do just that. The boy has learned to lead a double moral life.

The creator of the family system is the patriarch, Fyodor Mikhailovich. From behind the thin walls of his room, he seems to hear everything that is said in earshot and to learn of everything else.

He forces Lev to give back the 20 kopeks Bakhtin had given him for his drawing; he takes away the 19th-century banknote, the assignation, that Bakhtin had given the grandson; he refuses permission to Lev to leave his presence even for a day trip. With his withering, reproachful gaze, he controls everybody in the family. Bakhtin feels its power from the beginning; at their first meeting, the grandfather's "reproachful glance" tells Bakhtin that "it is no use to resist" being incorporated into the family system. Fyodor Mikhailovich complains bitterly about his posterity, declaring his sharp disappointment in both his son and his grandson, but he allows neither of them to have anything of his own. Everything that might be the independent possession of either is expropriated by the grandfather.

By the end of the story, we learn of the monstrous extreme to which Fyodor Mikhailovich has extended his expropriating grasp: he took his eldest son's wife away from him and, it is suggested, brought about the son's untimely death. We learn of the story from two of its participants. From Nikolai Fyodorovich we learn that the daughter-in-law in question was Lyudmila Grigoriyevna herself. He also says that he fell in love with her immediately. Lyudmila Grigoriyevna had told her story earlier in the third-person, concealing her role in it, but emphasizing the "conqueror's strength" of Fyodor Mikhailovich, such that "a woman who was then still quite young . . . without thinking . . . without shame . . . proudly looking people in the eye. . . . And Yuri Fyodorovich. . . . No, forgive me." Whether she breaks down here at the thought that her father-in-law got rid of his son when he appropriated his daughter-in-law is left ambiguous. However, the suggestion is clearly made. And even more clearly suggested is the consequence that Nikolay Fyodorovich married Lyudmila Grigoriyevna once Yuri was dead in obedience to the "system" of the Pavlov patriarch.

The final actor in this "system" is Lyudmila Grigoriyevna. We first see her as Bakhtin stumbles onto a highly unpleasant scene involving her and a local lover. Bakhtin sees her being slapped by the man, but before he can intervene, she has "instantaneously adopted a mask of tranquility." Her powers of dissimulation can be activated with lightning speed. She denies what Bakhtin has just witnessed with his own eyes. Later we understand her pathology better: it is the absence of a self. Her father-in-law having seduced her, she retains a memory of his "conqueror's strength." Living in an apparently sham marriage with Nikolai Fyodorovich, she is sexually available to the men in the town, and finally to Bakhtin himself. In keeping with the moral inversion characteristic of this family, her sexual encounter with Bakhtin comes about in the wake of a loud family row, which occurs due to the grandfather's conviction that the encounter has already taken place. She comes to Bakhtin to be consoled for her pain at being unjustly thought to have already had an affair with him—which leads to their affair actually occurring. And she understands that without the scandal, which Fyodor Mikhailovich had raised on the basis of the supposedly real affair, she "perhaps would not have come over" to Bakhtin. We are left with the suggestion that Fyodor Mikhailovich raised the scandal precisely to bring about the liaison with Bakhtin. Why did he do this? We are not told explicitly, but after Bakhtin first met Lyudmila Grigoriyevna and took in his first impression of her, he turned back to the house and "managed to catch the persistent and interested gaze of Fyodor Mikhailovich, who abruptly turned his eyes away."

This weirdly pathological family is not openly corrupt. The proprieties are strictly maintained: both the theft of the bicycle and the extramarital liaison with Bakhtin evoke loud moral protests. Voices are raised, doors slammed, punishments called for. The moral corruption of the family lies in the absence of self in any of its members except the hideous patriarch. Ultimately, that lack of self is due to the incestuous relationship on which, we learn, the family was founded. For Fyodor Mikhailovich has acted out a variant of the

Oedipus tragedy. He can be seen either as a successful Laius, getting rid of a son felt to be a competitor. Or he can be seen as a kind of reverse Oedipus, who directs his blind rage and lust downward in the generational tree toward his son and daughter-in-law instead of upward toward his father and mother. In either interpretation, he has transgressed against the limits that define a family. The result is a family group in which no one has a sense of self. No one, save the patriarch, can act independently. Beilis hints at the link between incest and a lack of self when he has Bakhtin immediately think of Oedipus in response to Lev's despair at not having a normal nickname. "The situation where name and nickname coincide suddenly appeared to him quite as awful as the situation of Oedipus after he discovers that his own children are also his siblings." In insisting that the 13-year-old boy bear the name and patronymic of a great writer and that he not have a more appropriate nickname, the grandfather transgresses onto the psychic space that should contain the growing boy's evolving sense of who he is. In Lev Nikolayevich's being forced to bear the name of the great, bearded Lev Tolstoy, he embodies in his name the collapse of the rightful distance between the generations—which is also the essence of Fyodor Mikhailovich's crime (and that of Oedipus). That collapse, which the Pavlovs show is consistent with a superficial maintenance of the proprieties, destroys the necessary precondition for the existence of an independent self, and in this story is shown to be profoundly incestuous.

BAKHTIN IN THE COUNTRY

Bakhtin's first reaction to the operation of the Pavlov family system occurs as he travels away from his first meeting with the family. When he realizes that as a result of the thinness of the walls (and of other means of communication) each member of the family seems to know what the guest told the other, "a wondrous sensation of mystery touched his soul." It is striking that Bakhtin, who will come to view the Pavlovs as "glued people" from whom he must detach himself, is at first drawn to precisely the lack of boundaries in that family. However, there is ambivalence in him. The "wondrous sensation of mystery" is "always surrounded by a sadness [that is] both exhausting and light." But in this case, the feeling is more than sadness: "a tension built up in his heart and communicated itself to his entire body nearly to the point of causing an involuntary muscular contraction." Thus a sweet sensation of mystery is followed by a tension that involves the whole body. In fact, Bakhtin will have to pass through the events of the entire summer before, at the end of the story, he will be able to articulate for himself the thought that is represented by this tension. The thought contained in this tension will find its first expression in a dream, and then will make its way to consciousness.

Bakhtin, though, at the moment of first feeling his ambivalent response to the Pavlovs, finds refuge from his "inadvertent and inexplicable uneasiness" in intellectual production. He thinks about his article. His meeting with the mysteriously joined Pavlovs has generated in him a concrete idea for his article. It is a Pirandellian notion according to which a literary character, in search of an Other in which to be realized, lodges in an author and is finally ejected through the author-host's "locking it up in the story as in a cage." Immediately after enjoying the activity of his mind in formulating this idea, Bakhtin obeys an impulse and takes a book from the shelf, finding a nearly identical formulation by M. M. Bakhtin. This makes him feel "ashamed and humiliated." Translating this experience of shame into the terms of his idea itself, a part of the I is suddenly exposed as being not-I; the psychic space that Bakhtin thinks is opening for him in his idea collapses suddenly and the result is acute embarrassment. This loss—an idea he thought was his suddenly turning out not to be his—then makes Bakhtin think of Fyodor

Mikhailovich, as of the ultimate cause of the loss. Bakhtin tries to regain some sense of self by seizing on the differences between his idea and that of his counterpart. This struggle sets off an even larger one in which "he himself resembled one possessed" and the possessing demon was none other than Fyodor Mikhailovich. Speaking the patriarch's name, Bakhtin feels that the demon has been exorcised, "and he felt himself drawn to the summer house." His summer is just beginning. He is still but scarcely differentiated from the Other.

On a walk in the forest, Bakhtin thinks up a game. He invents people and then imagines them as standing behind a tree, the game consisting in his guessing when the imaginary person will step out from behind the tree. One meaning of the game is his celebration of his mind's freedom. Not only is he creative in inventing individual people but his inventions are to some degree uncontrolled by Bakhtin himself. He thus finds a way—when deep in a forest far away from the village—to celebrate a freedom of the creative imagination that no member of the Pavlov family can be thought of as having. The game also reproduces the creative process of authorship, about which Bakhtin had been theorizing in such a conflicted way on his way back from his first meeting with the Pavlovs. Finally, in his game, Bakhtin is producing strangers who are not extensions of himself. They are not his doubles. In this way as well, he is reveling in a feature that sets him off from the Pavlovs.

Bakhtin's intellectual breakthrough comes in a delirium brought on by illness. He dreams of the "glued people" of Australian mythology, embryo-like beings attached to each other, which become human only when they are separated from each other and their eyes, mouth, and ears are opened by a knife; but the beings he dreams himself glued to are the Pavlovs, grandfather, father, wife, and grandson. His nightmare teaches him that what he "passionately desires" is "separateness and non-merging." This dream experience is clearly the climax of the story, the culmination of Bakhtin's summer with the Pavlov family, representing a kind of epiphany for the major character. It articulates the thought that was earlier represented unconsciously by the physical tension that accompanied Bakhtin's initial "wondrous sensation of mystery" upon first meeting the Pavlovs.

And yet it is no easy matter to find the will and understanding to assert separateness when one's life has been spent in various "glued" states. Beilis masterfully shows us the complexity of Bakhtin's situation by having him remember his dream only after being questioned about it by none other than Fyodor Mikhailovich himself. Only after the grandfather has asked him to explain certain foreign words, "inapatua" and "rella manerinia," which he has heard Bakhtin cry out in his delerium, does the latter remember his dream and become aware of its significance. He can appropriate this most important insight only after being prompted by the patriarch who stands at the head of the family from whom Bahktin so urgently desires to unglue himself. And as if to signal an already achieved inner separation in him, Bakhtin, upon being told about his delirious words, falls into thought and immediately wanders back into his room away from the grandfather, ignoring the latter who is still standing at the window and wanting to continue the conversation.

Later, armed with the insight provided by his dream, Bakhtin returns to the idea for his article. He had begun thinking about his article as an exploration of the differentiation of character from author. His dream presents a more personal version of that idea: his differentiation from the Pavlovs (and perhaps by extension from some need in himself for being "glued"). In the process, Bakhtin takes a stand diametrically opposed to the famous notion of his real counterpart. In seeing freedom in separation, he asserts that monologism is common consciousness, and dialogism is complete undifferentiation. By taking the central terms of M. M. Bakhtin and reversing their valuational sign, Bakhtin also announces a separation from his famous namesake.

VICTOR BEILIS AND RUSSIAN CULTURE

Although these two stories are quite different on the surface (in plot, major characters, intellectual background), important commonalities indicate the larger points Beilis is making, first, about Russian culture. Volodya and Lev Nikolayevich are both male teenagers who are stifled by overwhelming, internalized parental figures—mother and grandfather, respectively. Neither can have an emotional life that exists apart from these internalizations. Both are riven with anger at their situations, although they express this very differently. Volodya, despite his much greater psychological acumen, is nevertheless cut off from his anger in a way that his younger counterpart is not. Although he has highly explicit violent fantasies as a 14-year-old, in his adult years his anger recedes from awareness. Lev's conflicts, on the other hand, are closer to the surface. He acts them out—in outbursts, deceptions, and theft.

Irina Mikhailovna and Lyudmila Grigoriyevna are both married women who know how to combine an active extramarital sexual life with an established domesticity. Both have the inner flexibility to take advantage of their opportunities without undue strain. We see Lyudmila Grigoriyevna turn her emotions on a dime when she becomes aware of Bakhtin's approach during her painful conversation with a disappointed lover. Irina Mikhailovna is sexually and emotionally generous to Volodya in their first encounter, but that does not stop her from going into the bathroom to have sex with a stranger while at a party where Volodya is also present. In contrast to the profound inner constraint of the young men, these women demonstrate an absence of constraint that is impressive in its amorality.

We get closer to the center of the Beilis's vision of Russian culture in these stories when we note the centrality of incest to both worlds. Volodya is tormented by "delicious" incestuous fantasies, consciously as a young man and unconsciously as an older one. Incestuous desire seems so natural to him that it distorts his entire life, as we see in what he makes of his reading; for example, he does not see anything wrong in *planning* to enjoy fantasied surrogate incest with his future mother-in-law.

The Pavlov family is itself founded on an act of incest. The grandfather, Fyodor Mikhailovich, took his oldest son's wife for himself, and possibly got rid of the son. He may well be Lev Nikolayevich's real father. The lack of independent selves in the family is ultimately a consequence of this act. Incest destroys the self. Acted out by Fyodor Mikhailovich, it leaves his family devoid of independent selves. They are all doubles, reflections, of the transgressing patriarch.

Thus Beilis gives us a vision of life profoundly compromised by incest. These two stories represent in one sense a thinking through of the consequences of incest. Their amoral women have accommodated themselves to a world distorted by incest. Lyudmila Grigoriyevna still speaks with emotion of her father-in-law lover's "conqueror's strength," and Irina Mikhailovna clearly enjoys her dalliance with Volodya, who is so much younger than she that even her jaded coworkers are shocked. Indeed, accommodation to a life compromised by incest to a large degree defines these women's amorality. Conversely, the neurotic young men are deeply flawed by their guilt-ridden adaptation to an incest-corrupted world. Volodya dies at the moment his life is about to become normal, a victim of his unacknowledged feeling of guilt, and Lev Nikolayevich seems permanently confused about his identity. Volodya cannot separate the women he is with from (an unconscious fantasy of) his mother. Lev cannot separate the older men he comes into contact with from his grandfather (who may really be his father).

Ultimately, Beilis gives us a vision of a Russian culture that devours individuals. In this critical vision, incestuous feelings exert a ferocious power in opposition to the separation that defines an individual. One reflection of this cultural critique is the narrower critique of the work of Mikhail Mikhailovich Bakhtin, whose key notion of dialogism is dismissed by the fictional Bakhtin as "complete undifferentiation." For Russia, Beilis is saying, to celebrate dialogue, understood as the formation of selves through other selves, is to endanger the idea of the individual (just as it was, we might now add, to celebrate collectivism, understood as the subordination of selves to the group). For without the individual, what kind of self can there be?

Lack of differentiation, in "Bakhtin and Others," is of course demonstrated on one level by the "bacchanalia of names" in the story, beginning with Bakhtin's own name. However, the comic effect of a family whose members bear the names and patronymics of Dostoyevsky and Tolstoy should not distract us from Beilis's deeper point about the hostility of Russian culture to the individual. The comedy of non-differentiating names also refers to the pathology of this incestuous, "glued" family. Just as they are "glued" by their family history of incest, their names (which, we recall, are planned for two more generations) also demonstrate their lack of healthy separation from each other and from their culture. It is important to note that the family fixation on writers' names begins with Lev Nikolayevich, the product of the old man's incestuous passion. The old man's other sons bear non-literary names.

Volodya, for his part, also bears a famous name, one that resounds in modern Russian history. The reference in the young man's name to Vladimir Ilich Lenin (Volodya being the usual nickname for Vladimir) is perhaps less obvious to the naked eye than the Pavlovs' names but runs far deeper and indicates another area of implied meaning in the story. For Volodya's reading of Freud exactly parallels Lenin's reading of Marx. Both find in a Western *theory* a guide to *action*. And both end up with wildly distorted readings of the texts precisely because they crave action. In Volodya's case, Freud's theory of the unconscious incestuous currents between sons- and mothers-in-law is distorted into yielding a means for experiencing incestuous pleasures. In Lenin's case, Marx's theory of world proletarian revolution was distorted into yielding a plan for bringing about a proletarian revolution in a country without a proletariat. Both Volodyas, excited and emboldened by Western theory, acted on their passion—blindly, enthusiastically, ignorantly, and, in both cases, with disastrous results. Therefore, in giving us one Volodya blinded by incestuous passion, Beilis invites us to consider an incestuous meaning behind the actions of the other Volodya, who, as we know, took possession of Mother Russia and had his way with her.

VICTOR BEILIS AND INDIVIDUATION

These two stories come together most generally in the theme of individuation, which in both is seen as requiring a separation. Volodya strives to free himself from his crippling emotional tie to his mother. On the conscious plane, he succeeds in separating. On the unconscious plane, he does not succeed, and his failure is marked by his recurring depression and self-doubt. On the story's final page, the unconscious tie overwhelms the conscious separation. Because he has no way to deal with his unconscious tie, not even a language with which to describe it, he can only see what is on the surface of his life, and the surface always shows him progress and victories. This young Russian man, although perhaps living closer to his unconscious than an American counterpart, does not have access either to the idea of unconscious processes or to the profession that could help him understand them in himself. Thus, not aware of the level at which he remains tied, he fails to separate.

Bakhtin succeeds where Volodya fails, after a fashion. He does separate, at least within the much more limited frame of a story about an intellectual who sets out to write an article. We have traced the process by which he arrives at his separation. An initial attraction to the Pavlovs is accompanied by a physical tension, a feeling that is finally articulated in his dream of cutting himself away from "glued people" using a Finnish knife, and of thus achieving differentiation. Two elements in this process distinguish his fate from Volodya's. First, in Bakhtin's dream, the act of cutting himself loose from the attached beings is bloody, violent, and painful. We see that separation requires the willingness to inflict pain on oneself and others in the self-conscious, determined effort to be free. Volodya, despite the discipline and intelligence of his effort at self-cure, always finds his cure in the next incarnation of his mother, and thus never undergoes the pain of loosening that tie.

Second, Bakhtin only becomes aware of his dream at all as a result of Fyodor Mikhailovich, who through the wall has heard him cry out certain foreign words and later asks him about them. Thus the indispensable facilitator of Bakhtin's epiphany is none other than the monstrous grandfather himself. The irony of this indispensability aside, the key here to linking the conscious and the unconscious planes for Bakhtin is the intervention of another person. The indispensability of the intervention is shown by the fact that, even after Bakhtin has explained for the grandfather the meaning of the words "rella manerinia" and "inapatua," he still does not remember his dream until the grandfather tells him how he came to hear them. Then Bakhtin becomes so lost in thought he walks away from the other in the middle of their conversation.

Volodya certainly has intense erotic dreams about his mother, and yet, perhaps because they occur during his adolescence and thus while his mind is still forming, they do not provide him with the kind of liberating information that Bakhtin's dream does for him. Tormented by his dreams and by his failures with women, Volodya first tries to find an advising Other in Freud's books. But his reading results in nothing more than a strange plan to find a mother-in-law to fall in love with. Irina, in their first encounter, attempts to play the role of the advising Other, going so far as to leave a message in the form of a quotation from Pushkin: "He, a handsome man, imagined himself hideous and avoided the company of people unfamiliar to him, intimidated by their mocking glances." Viewed in the context of Volodya's entire fate, the quotation reveals a profound psychological intuition on Irina's part. For Volodya, everyone's favorite at work and at parties, is indeed quite unaware of how hideous he finds himself in his unconscious life. If Volodya were able to appreciate the significance of Irina's message, he might have a different fate. But instead of understanding the sense in which she was profoundly right, he proceeds to torment himself with paranoid thoughts that end in wondering if she was dissatisfied with the duration of their sexual act.

Seen together in this way, these two stories present readers with two visions of the serious business of individuation. In their different ways, and despite the delightful humor in both, they show that individuation is a life-and-death matter. It is achieved, or not, in opposition to lethal forces. For Russian readers of these stories in 1992, the year after the end of the Soviet Union, one meaning of this theme was that the most powerful forces arrayed against individuation are found not in uniforms but in psyches. For 21st-century American readers, people for whom individuation has long since become a commonplace of law and commerce, this theme can be a reminder, and not the first such to come out of Russia, of how serious a thing the individual is.

R.B.G.

BIBLIOGRAPHY

AND

SUGGESTED READING

———————

Clark, K., and Holquist, M. *Mikhail Bakhtin.* Cambridge, MA: Belknap
Press of Harvard University Press.

Etkind, A. *Eros of the Impossible: The History of Psychoanalysis in Russia,*
trans. N. Rubins and M. Rubins. Boulder, CO, and Oxford: Westview
Press, division of HarperCollins.

Miller, M. *Freud and the Bolsheviks.* New Haven, CT, and London: Yale
University Press.

Rice, J. *Freud's Russia: National Identity in the Evolution of Psychoanalysis.*
New Brunswick, NJ, and London: Transaction Publishers.

ABOUT THE AUTHOR

Victor Beilis was born in 1943 in the part of the Soviet Union then known as the Turkmen Soviet Socialist Republic, now the independent country of Turkmenia, which borders on Iran, Afghanistan, Uzbekistan, and Kazakhstan. His parents, who at the time of his birth were still university students, had been evacuated to that remote Soviet republic from their native Odessa to escape the destruction of World War II. After the war, the family lived in Lvov (now Lviv), Ukraine, where his father was a professor of history and his mother a biology teacher. Literature was among his first interests in school, especially Shakespeare and the Ancient Greeks. In 1961, upon graduation from high school, he entered the Moscow Institute of Oriental Languages where he concentrated on African languages and cultures.

Beilis has published many books and articles on African culture, including works on the Nobel laureate Wole Soyinka, the African idea of the city, and African mythology, rituals, and literature. But in the years before glasnost, while these works were appearing, Beilis was also writing fiction and plays. In 1992, he published a volume containing four works, two of which were "The Rehabilitation of Freud" and "Bakhtin and Others." In 1993, Beilis emigrated from Russia, settling in Frankfurt, Germany, where he now lives with his wife. He currently teaches courses in African culture at the University of Frankfurt. He has a son who is married, lives in Japan, and recently made him a grandfather.